START PLAYING KEYBOARD
OMNIBUS EDITION:BOOKS 1 & 2

by Peter Lavender

Wise Publications
part of The Music Sales Group
London/New York/Paris/Sydney/Copenhagen/Berlin/Madrid/Hong Kong/Tokyo

Arranged and compiled by Peter Lavender.
Music processed by Hillmob Music Services.

Printed in the EU.

Part 1

Keyboard music basics, and the easy-to-read
SFX 'letter-note' music system

Part 2

Fingered chord technique. Easy transition from
SFX 'letter-note' to standard music notation

SFX – SOUNDS 'n' EFFECTS PART 1

About This Book

Welcome to SFX music.

When you play music the SFX way, you become a performing musician almost from the word 'go'. That's because SFX music is easy to read . . . quick to learn . . . and fun to play. What's more, there are SFX music books to suit all tastes and for all occasions.

Before you start, here are a few tips which you will find useful:

Always use the right sound, the right rhythm and the right tempo. The choice of these settings depends on the particular tune you are playing. For instance, you wouldn't put a 'brassy' sound suitable for a march with a gentle waltz. So whenever you play a song, always decide on registrations which fit. A change in the tempo of the rhythm changes the character of a piece of music. Always keep the tempo down to a reasonable speed until you've mastered the melody. And never play a background effect so loud that it over-rides the melody.

Follow the suggested registrations in this book along with rhythm and tempo settings. They are a starting guide while you learn and enjoy playing SFX music.

Finally, get to know all the Sounds 'n' Effects on your keyboard. Explore these exciting features from the start. Vary the sounds and rhythms every time you play the tunes through.

Have Fun.

All keyboard instruments have the same layout of black and white keys.

The black keys are arranged in alternate groups of 2 and 3 notes:

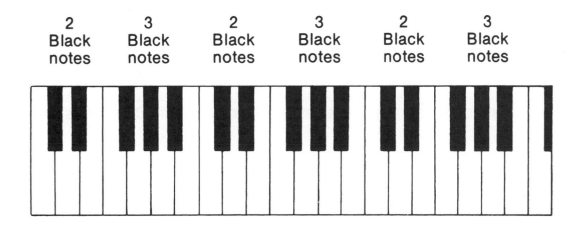

| 2 Black notes | 3 Black notes | 2 Black notes | 3 Black notes | 2 Black notes | 3 Black notes |

A melody played on the keyboard is a sequence of musical tones. Each of these tones can be written as **music notes** on and around the **staff**.

The staff (or "Stave" as it is sometimes called) has 5 **lines** and 4 **spaces**.

A treble clef sign is placed at the beginning of the first staff in all SFX music to indicate that the notes are for right hand melody playing:

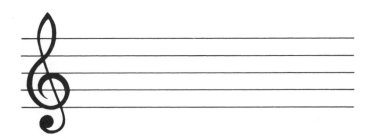

Each line and space has a letter name by which music notes appearing in the staff are identified.

To help you to play your favourite tunes straight away, all music notes in SFX songbooks show their letter names.

This makes SFX music as simple as

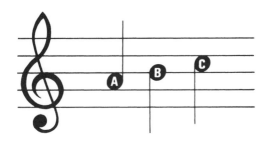

In music the first seven letters of the alphabet are used, and this is how they appear in SFX notes:

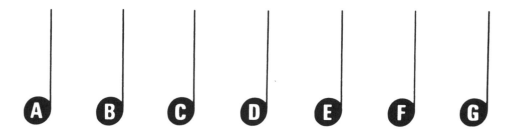

In SFX songbooks, most of the tunes use notes from middle C upwards on your keyboard.

Middle C is in the centre area of the keyboard, immediately left of two black keys:

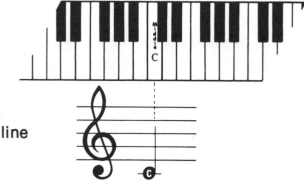

The middle C note is written just below the staff. A short line (called a Ledger Line) cuts through the note head.

The first 5 right hand melody notes, starting from Middle C, go up the keyboard and up the staff.

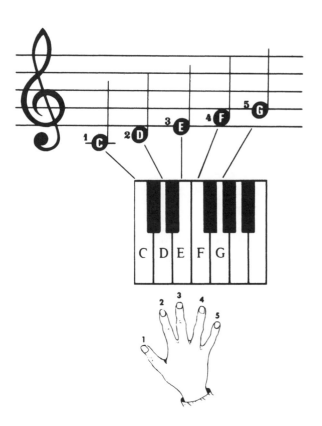

Position your right hand just above the keyboard, with a slight downward curve of the fingers. Starting with the thumb (finger number 1), play Middle C. Release the key then play the next note D (finger 2), release, and on to E (finger 3), F (finger 4), and lastly G with the 5th finger.

Repeat this several times to get the feel of the keys. Try to keep your eyes on each note of music in the staff as you play its key.

Now reverse the sequence. Starting on G (5th finger), play each note in turn, back down to Middle C.

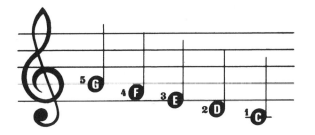

Finally, play all five notes **up** and then back **down** again. Important playing 'pointers': keep your eyes on the music, don't let your hand sag at the wrist, and play all the notes evenly with an equal sounding time for each tone.

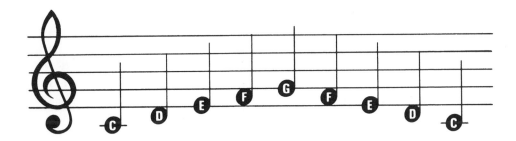

Music notes. There are three main types of music notes, each having a *time value* that is counted in regular **beats**:

The WHOLE NOTE = ○ = 4 BEATS

The HALF NOTE = = 2 BEATS

The QUARTER NOTE = = 1 BEAT

Bar lines are vertical lines that appear throughout the staff. The distance between two bar lines is called a **measure**. Each measure contains a fixed number of beats depending on the type of music. A double bar line is always placed at the end of a piece of music:

The time signature always appears at the beginning of the music. It tells you the number of beats in each measure, and the type of note that will represent one beat.

The top number in the time signature shows the amount of beats in each measure.

The bottom number indicates the type of note that will have *one* beat. In this "Four-four" time signature, the lower 4 represents the *Quarter Note*.

All other types of notes that occur in the "Four-four" time will be governed by the Quarter Note time value of one beat:

4 Quarter Notes to the measure

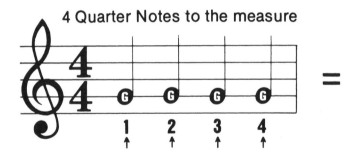

2 Half Notes to the measure

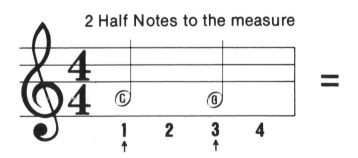

1 Whole Note to the measure

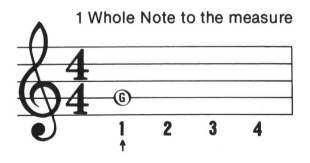

Some well known tunes can now be played on your keyboard using the notes learned so far.

Play the first five melodies with your *right hand only*, using the fingering marked alongside the notes. Take care to give each note its correct time value — the beat count is given in the first few measures.

When you have become familiar with playing these tunes with the right hand, the *left hand accompaniment* can be added.

The following letters appear above the music staff:

These are the names of **chords**. A chord is several musical tones sounding together, providing accompaniment to the melody. By simply playing the appropriate key in the chord section of the keyboard with your left hand, the instrument will automatically produce this accompaniment.

Your Owner's Manual will fully explain the automatic chord function and other similar features programmed into the keyboard.

Au Clair De La Lune

Traditional

Suggested Registration:
PIANO
or
FLUTE

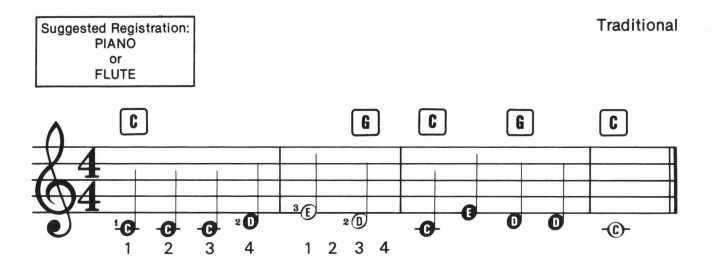

Largo

by Antonin Dvorak

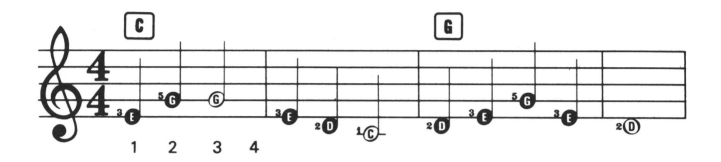

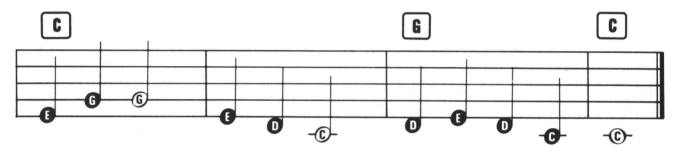

Merrily We Roll Along

Traditional

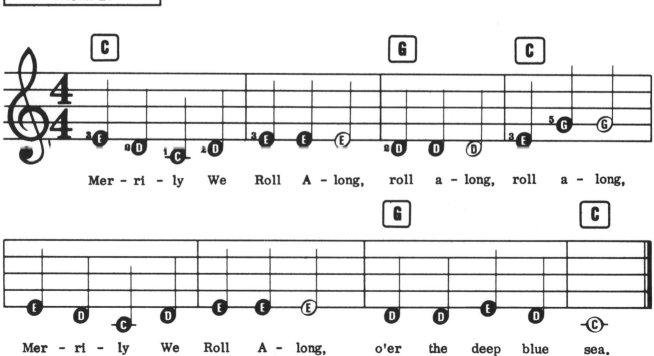

Mer - ri - ly We Roll A - long, roll a - long, roll a - long,

Mer - ri - ly We Roll A - long, o'er the deep blue sea.

The next song introduces the "7th" type of chord: **G** 7

When using automatic chord accompaniment, your Owner's Manual will explain the simple two-finger left hand key position that produces 7th chords.

If the 7th chord is not programmed into your keyboard, disregard the figure 7 appearing outside the chord symbol box — the basic chord will provide adequate accompaniment to the melody.

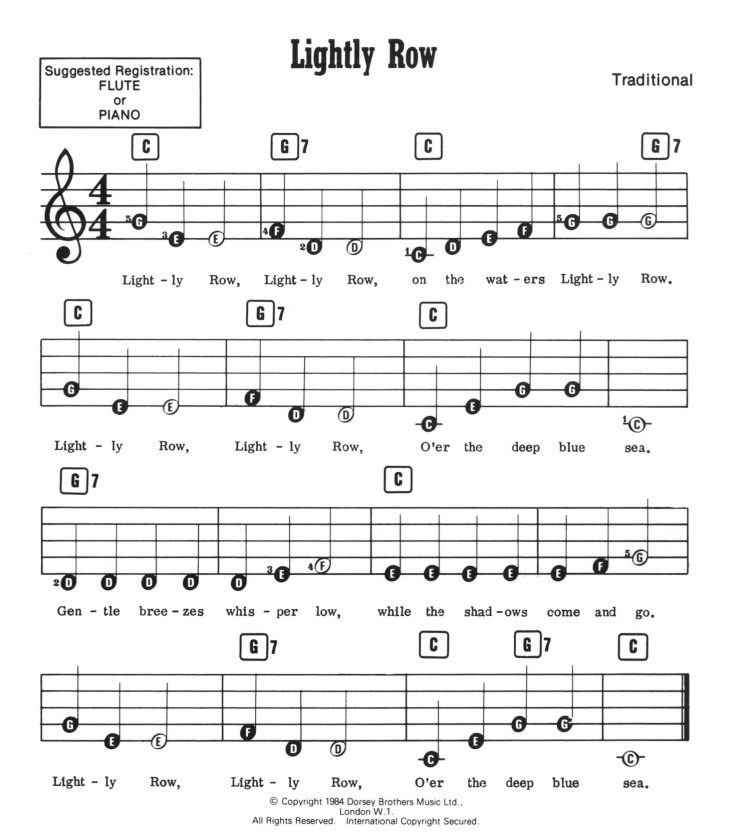

Lightly Row

Traditional

Suggested Registration:
FLUTE
or
PIANO

Light - ly Row, Light - ly Row, on the wat - ers Light - ly Row.

Light - ly Row, Light - ly Row, O'er the deep blue sea.

Gen - tle bree - zes whis - per low, while the shad - ows come and go.

Light - ly Row, Light - ly Row, O'er the deep blue sea.

Jingle Bells

Traditional

Suggested Registration:
VIBRAPHONE
or
CHIMES

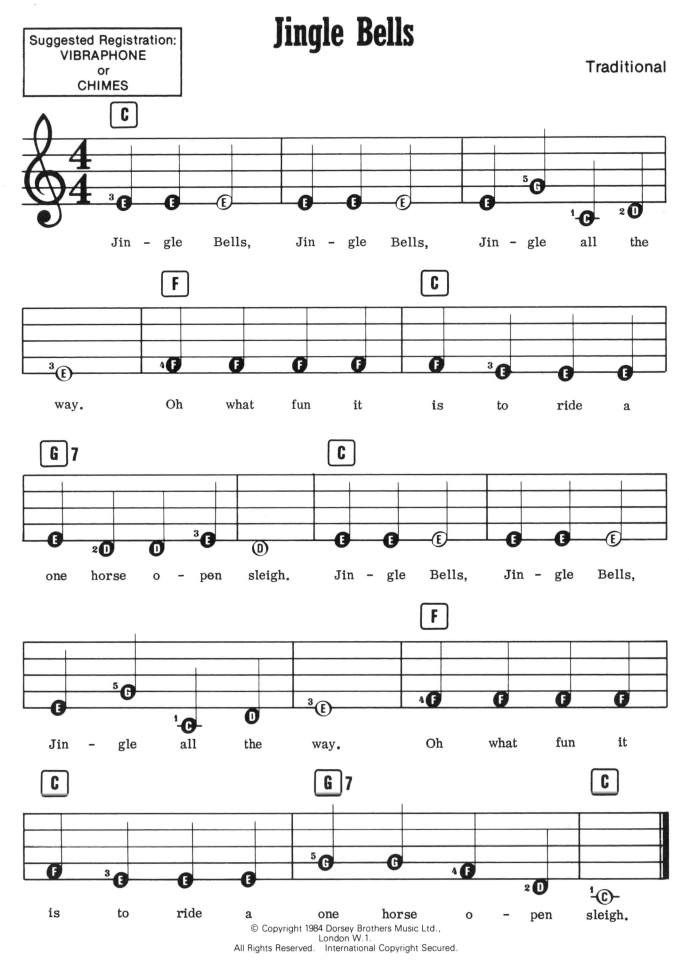

Jin - gle Bells, Jin - gle Bells, Jin - gle all the way. Oh what fun it is to ride a one horse o - pen sleigh. Jin - gle Bells, Jin - gle Bells, Jin - gle all the way. Oh what fun it is to ride a one horse o - pen sleigh.

When you have played these tunes through with chord accompaniment, try adding **rhythm**. Your Owner's Manual will explain this feature.

Set the *Tempo* at **medium** speed, with **swing**, **soft rock**, or similar 'four-to-the-measure' pattern.

Waltz time is often referred to as "three-four time", as can be seen from the popular waltz time signature:

This time signature indicates there are 3 Quarter Notes, each with a beat, in every measure:

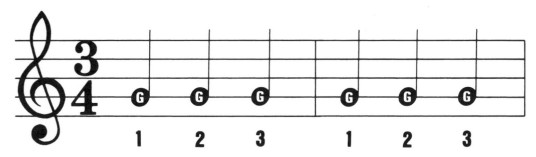

The Dotted Half Note. When a dot is placed after a note, the *time value* of that note is increased by one-half of its value. The Dotted Half Note therefore has a count of 3 beats:

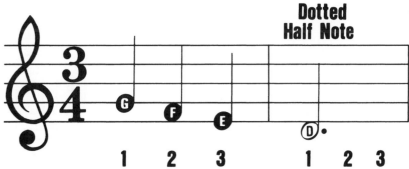

The Tie is a curved line that links consecutive notes on the same line or in the same space of the staff. When a tie appears in the music, play the first note and sustain the sound for the full time value of the tied note sequence:

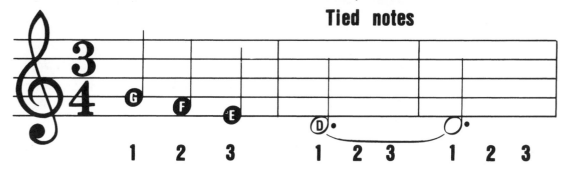

Barcarolle

by Jacques Offenbach

| Suggested Registration: CLASSICAL ORGAN or STRINGS | Rhythm: WALTZ | Tempo: MEDIUM |

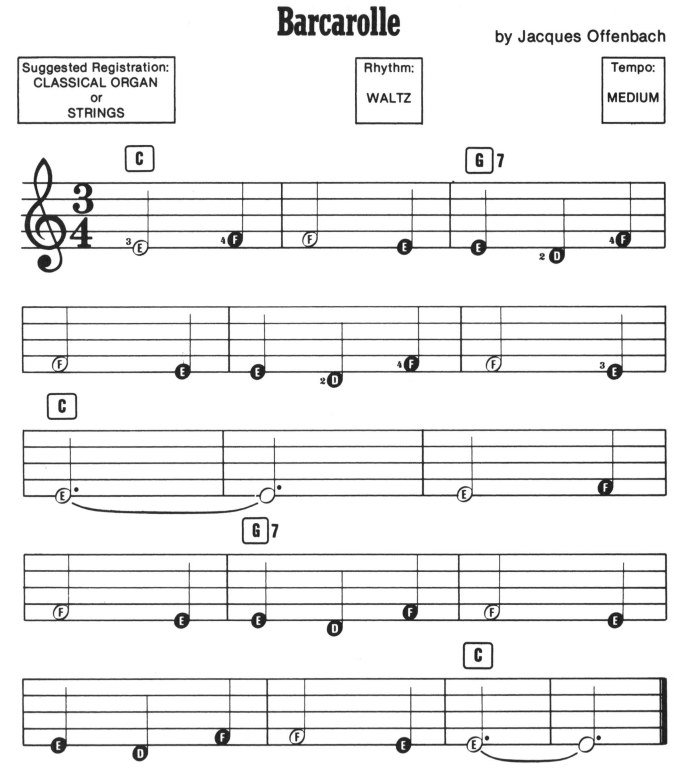

Pick Up Notes occur when a piece of music starts with one or several notes that do not total a full measure. They are played at their usual time value. In most cases the last measure of music rounds everything off by supplying the missing beat. A double bar line usually follows Pick Up Notes.

The words NO CHORD sometimes appear above Pick Up Notes indicating they are best played without accompaniment. This is when the RHYTHM "SYNCHRO" feature on your keyboard can be used most effectively. The Pick Up Notes are played without rhythm, and the "Synchro" feature will start the rhythm immediately you add the chord accompaniment.

The old jazz favourite "When The Saints Go Marching In" begins with three Quarter Notes in 4/4 time signature.

When The Saints Go Marching In

Traditional

Suggested Registration:	Tempo:	Rhythm:
TRUMPET or JAZZ ORGAN	MEDIUM	SWING

16

The next songs introduce three new notes in the music staff — A, B and C:

By using the fingering marked alongside music notes in these songs, your right hand melody playing will develop a smooth and confident playing style.

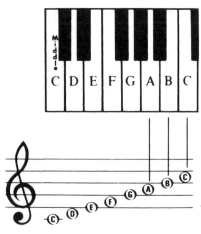

Michael Row The Boat Ashore

Traditional

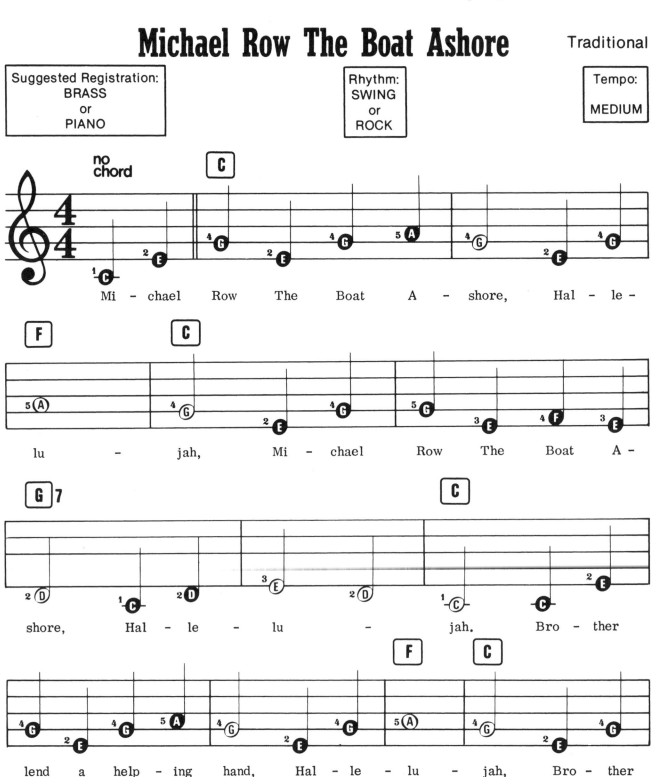

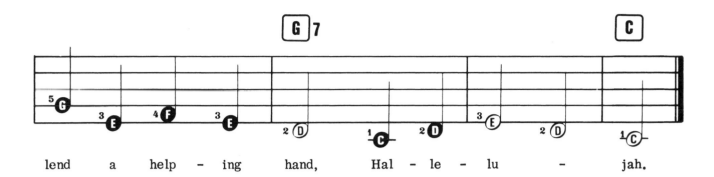

lend a help - ing hand, Hal - le - lu - jah.

She Wore A Yellow Ribbon

Traditional

| Suggested Registration: GUITAR or TRUMPET | Rhythm: SWING or MARCH | Tempo: MEDIUM |

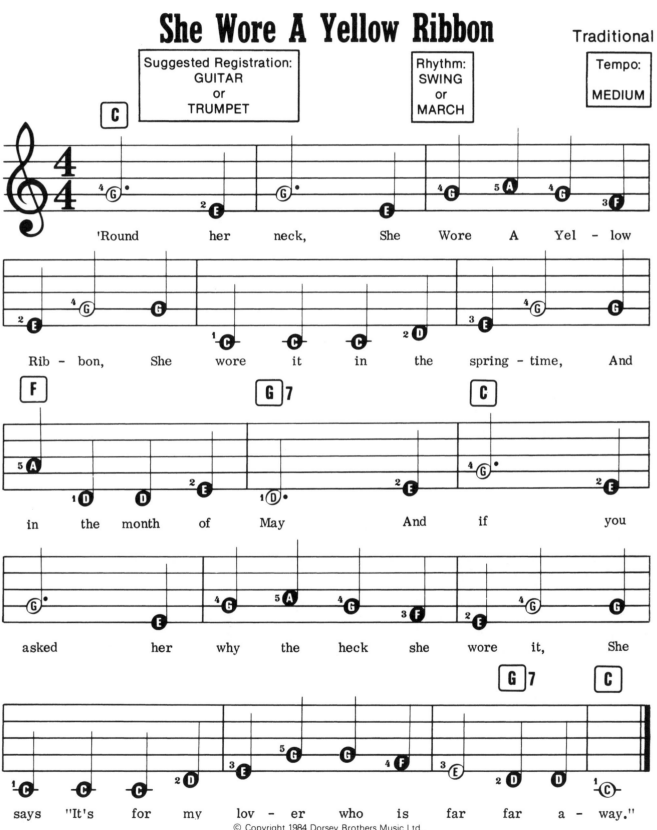

'Round her neck, She Wore A Yel - low
Rib - bon, She wore it in the spring - time, And
in the month of May And if you
asked her why the heck she wore it, She
says "It's for my lov - er who is far far a - way."

Repeat signs are often used in a song when a part or sometimes all of the melody is to be played through again. They save space and unnecessary turning of pages:

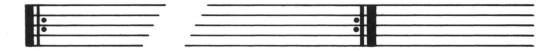

All music appearing between the Repeat Signs is to be replayed.

The word **fine** in the last measure of this song means 'End' — the point to finish playing after the Repeat has been made.

On Top Of Old Smoky

Traditional

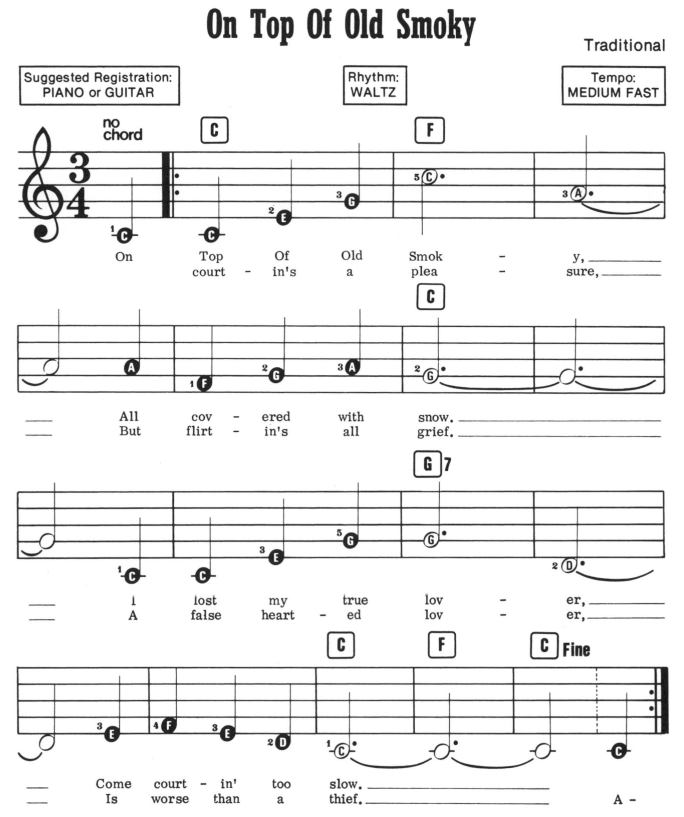

Quite often there will only be one Repeat Sign that appears at the end of a section of music. The repeat is then made from the very beginning:

Chopsticks

Traditional

| Suggested Registration: XYLOPHONE or PIANO | Rhythm: WALTZ | Tempo: FAST |

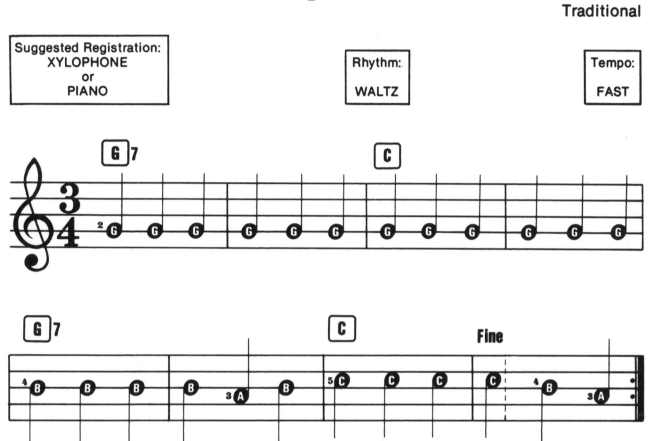

Double Endings. Sometimes a change in the melody will occur for one or several measures towards the end of a repeat section of music. Double Endings, using 1st and 2nd time brackets above the staff, mark off where a short 'skip' is to be made after the repeat has been played through:

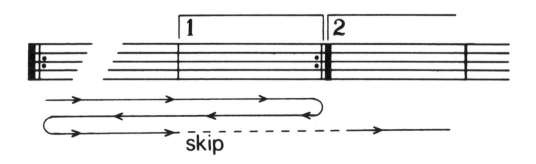

Wooden Heart

Words & Music by
Fred Wise, Ben Weisman,
Kay Twomey & Berthold Kaempfert

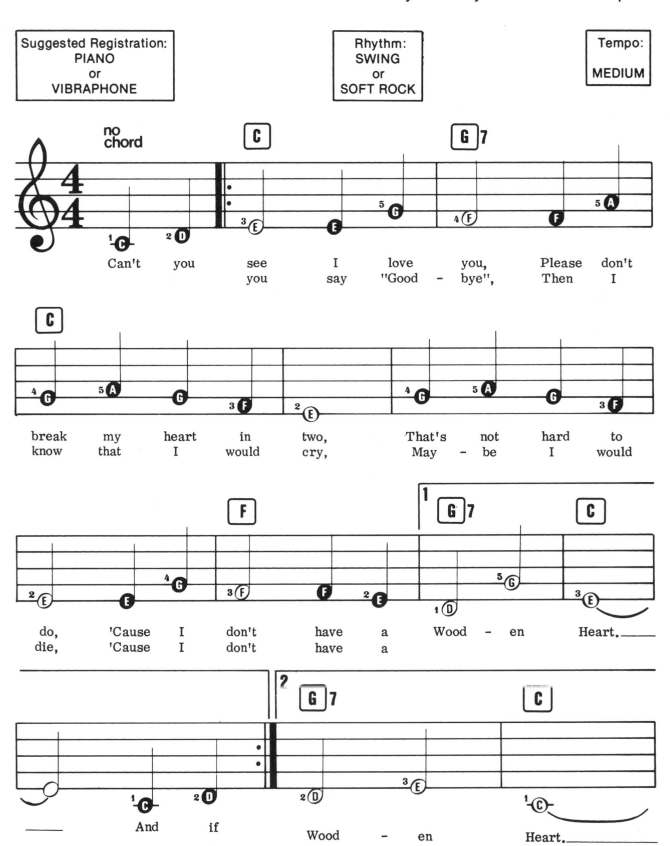

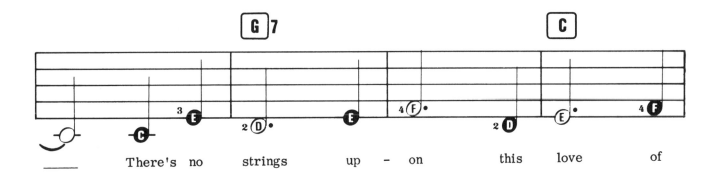

There's no strings up - on this love of

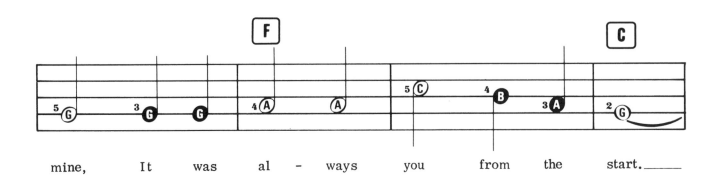

mine, It was al - ways you from the start.____

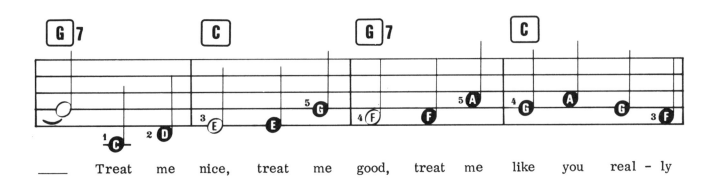

____ Treat me nice, treat me good, treat me like you real - ly

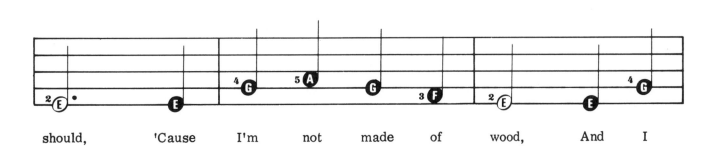

should, 'Cause I'm not made of wood, And I

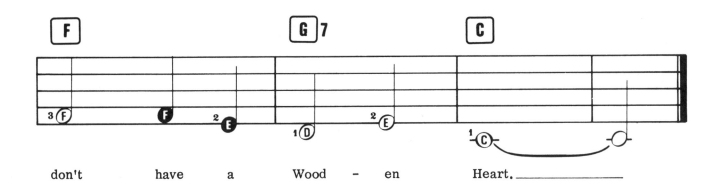

don't have a Wood - en Heart._____

The "Can Can" has a series of notes running down in the 7th and 8th measures. Try to get a smooth cross-fingering between the notes F and E in the 8th measure.

The Can Can

by Jacques Offenbach

| Suggested Registration: BRASS or VIBRAPHONE | Rhythm: SWING or ROCK | Tempo: MEDIUM FAST |

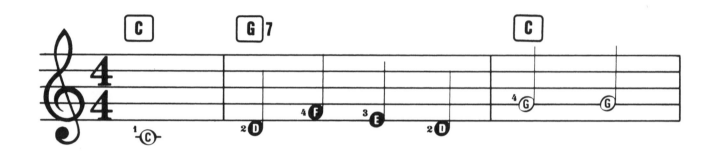

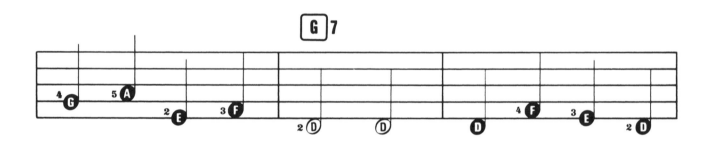

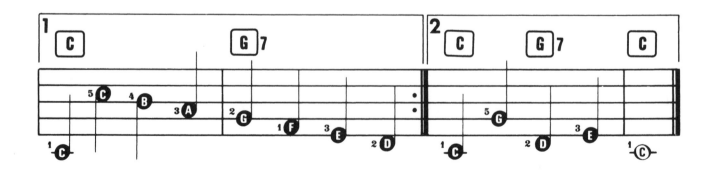

Five new notes continue up the staff, with a ledger line for the last note:

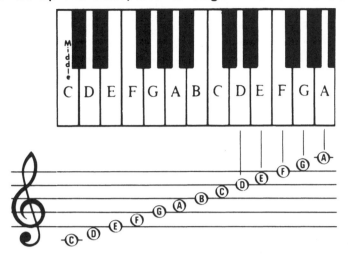

She'll Be Coming 'Round The Mountain

Traditional

| Suggested Registration: BANJO or XYLOPHONE | Rhythm: SWING | Tempo: FAST |

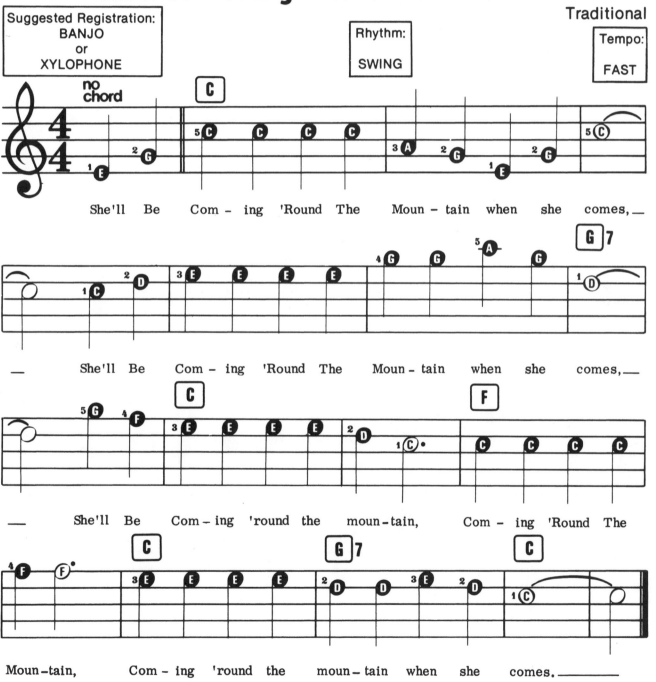

Where Have All The Flowers Gone

Words & Music by
Pete Seeger

Suggested Registration: FLUTE or STRINGS	Rhythm: BEGUINE/RHUMBA or SOFT ROCK	Tempo: MEDIUM

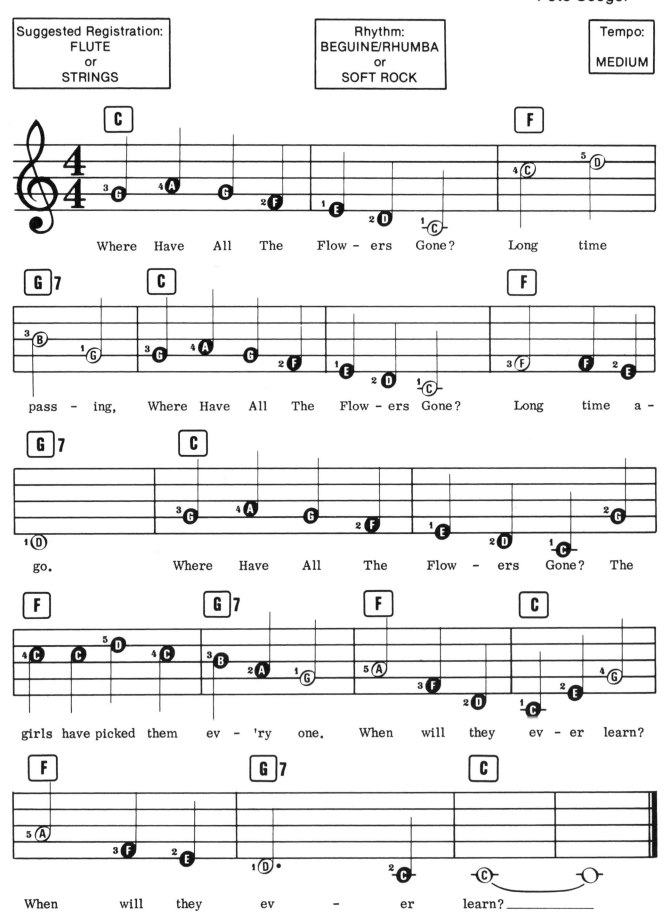

This song introduces a new chord: **D**7

Love Me Tender

Words & Music by
Elvis Presley & Vera Matson

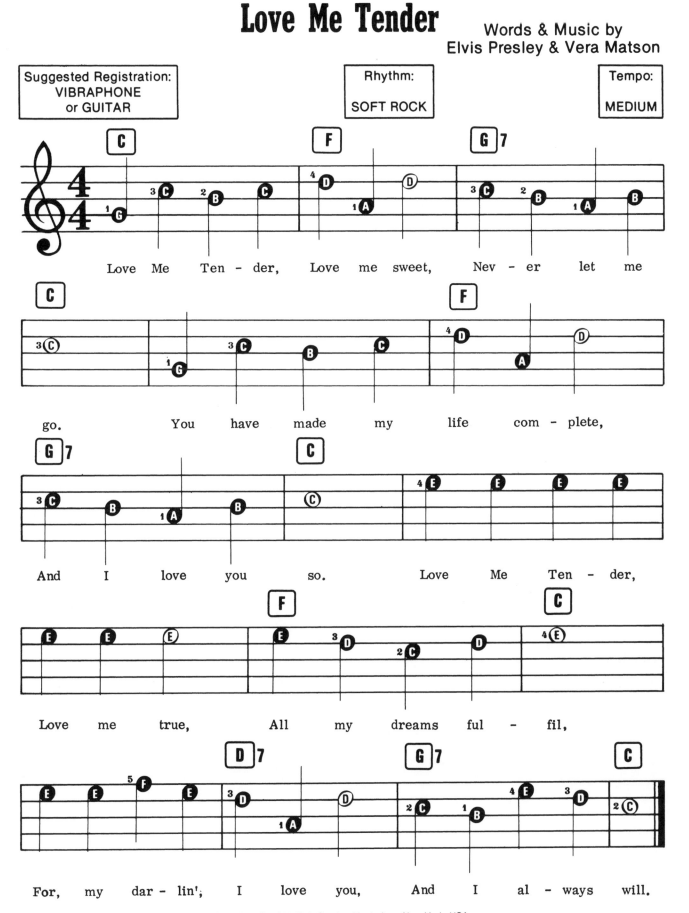

Snow Waltz

Traditional

| Suggested Registration: VIBRAPHONE or PIANO | Rhythm: WALTZ | Tempo: MEDIUM FAST |

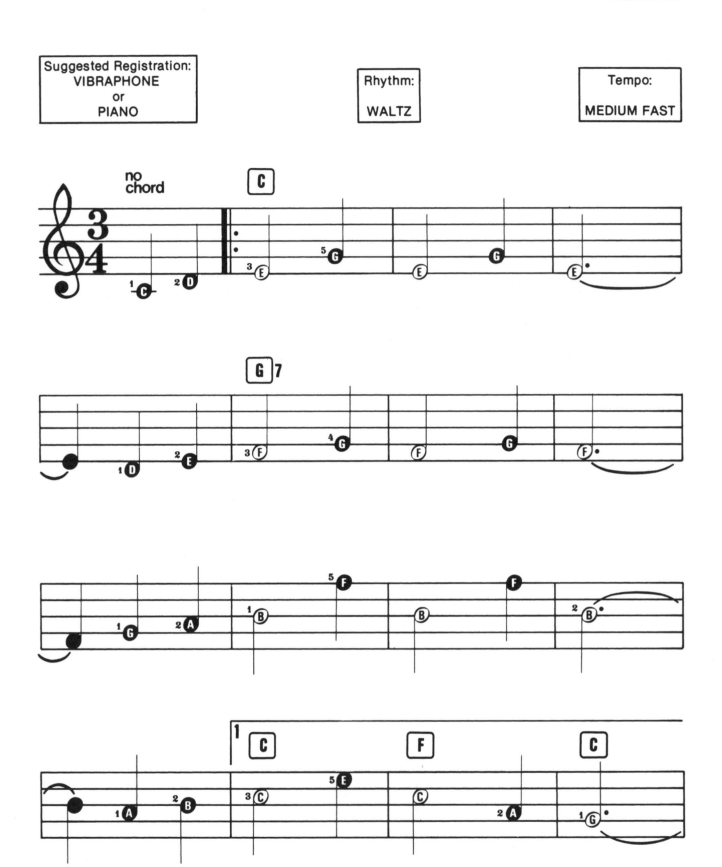

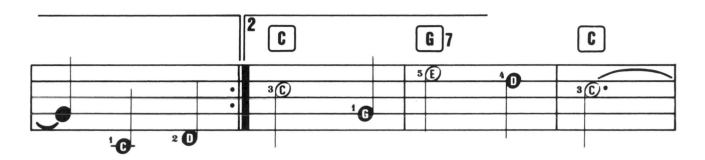

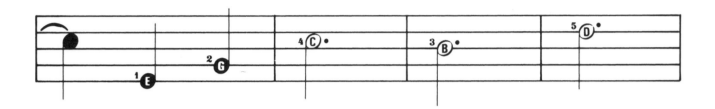

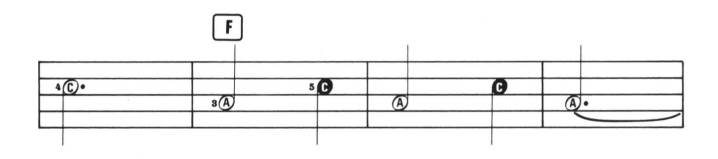

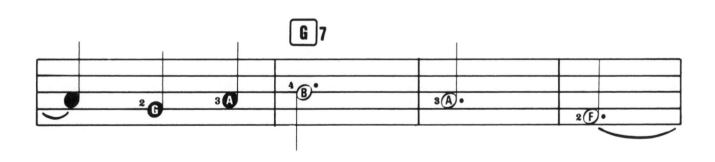

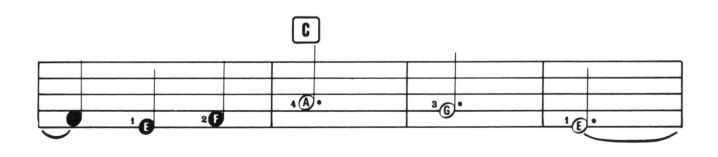

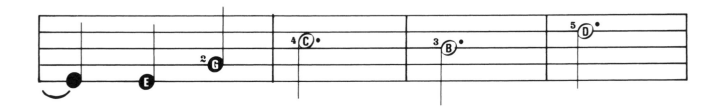

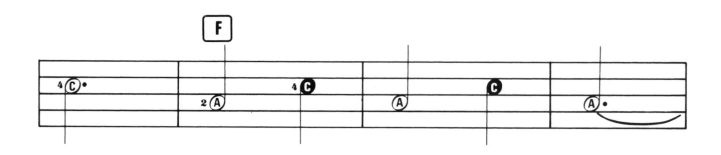

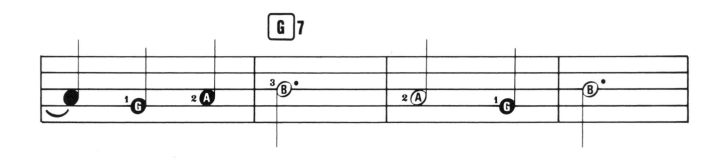

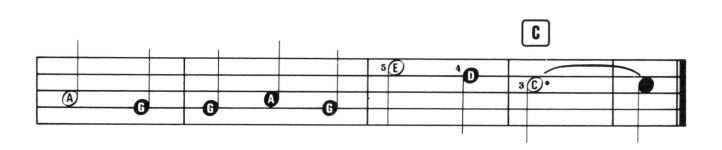

Everyone's Gone To The Moon

Words & Music by
Jonathan King

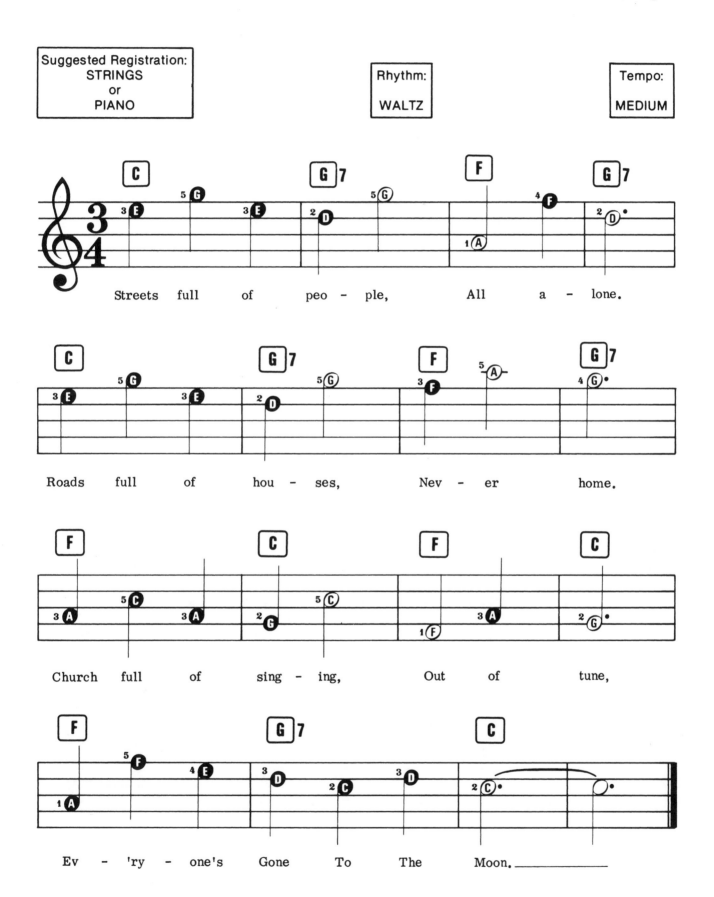

The Eighth Note has a tail:

In pairs, and groups of 4, the tails become *beams*:

The Eighth Note has a time value that is one-half of a Quarter Note. A pair of Eighth Notes therefore equal one Quarter Note:

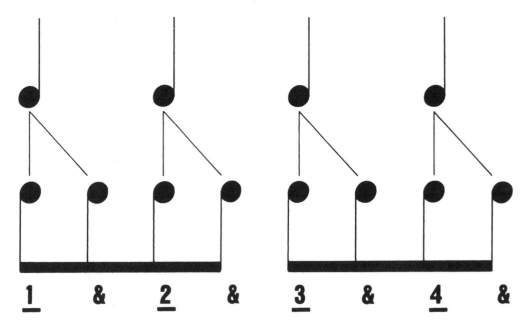

The "&" used in the Eighth Note count is one way to split the Quarter Note beat.

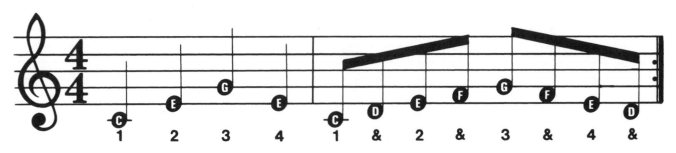

Another method is to tap your foot in time to the beat. Each down-and-up movement of the toe is a pair of Eighth Notes forming 1 beat.

Skip To My Lou

Traditional

Birdie Song/Birdie Dance

Words & Music by
Werner Thomas & Terry Rendall

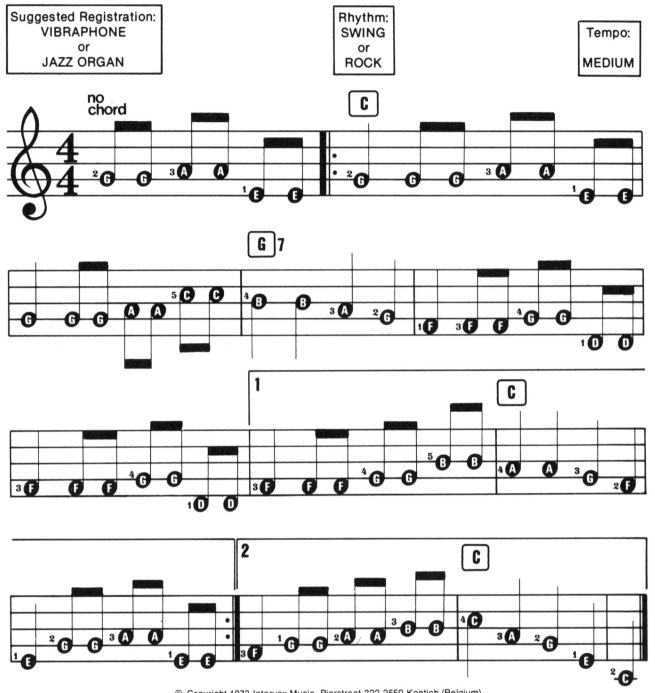

The Dotted Quarter Note.
When a dot appears after the
Quarter Note, its value is
increased by one half:

= 1 beat, + "½ for the dot"
= 1½ **beats.**

The Dotted Quarter Note is
usually followed by an Eighth
Note to make a full two-beat
phrase:

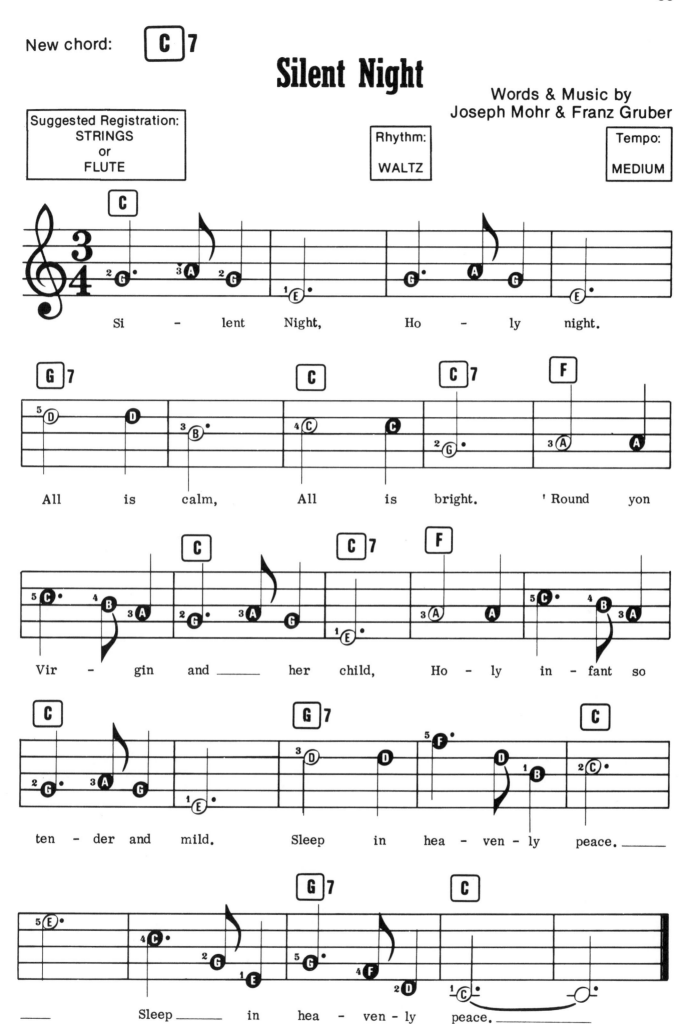

Rests. All our music so far has been a variety of different sounding notes, with a mixture of note values to give rhythm to the flow of musical sounds.

There are moments in all kinds of music however, when a complete silence is briefly needed. These rests are also handy for the casual fingering or "sound" change!

Rests are musical symbols that are written in the staff, and like music notes, each rest has a time value:

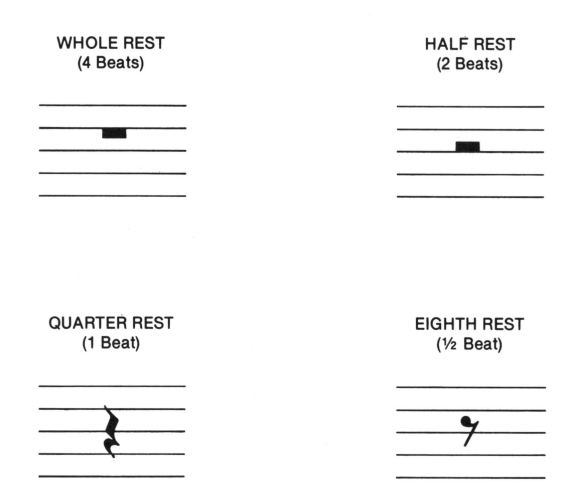

WHOLE REST
(4 Beats)

HALF REST
(2 Beats)

QUARTER REST
(1 Beat)

EIGHTH REST
(½ Beat)

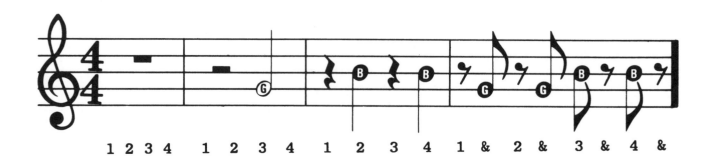

Gonna Build A Mountain

Words & Music by
Leslie Bricusse & Anthony Newley

Minor Chords. The next song introduces the *Minor* chords:

When using automatic chord accompaniment, your Keyboard Owner's Manual will explain the simple two-finger key position in the left hand that produces Minor chord accompaniment.

Sailing

Words & Music by
Gavin Sutherland

Sharps and flats. By the occasional use of the black notes on your keyboard, SFX music now opens up the way for you to play all the great songs in the SFX music books.

This music symbol is the **sharp**:

When it appears just before a note, simply play the *black key* that lies immediately to the *right* of the white key.

This has the effect of **sharp**ening the musical pitch of the written note:

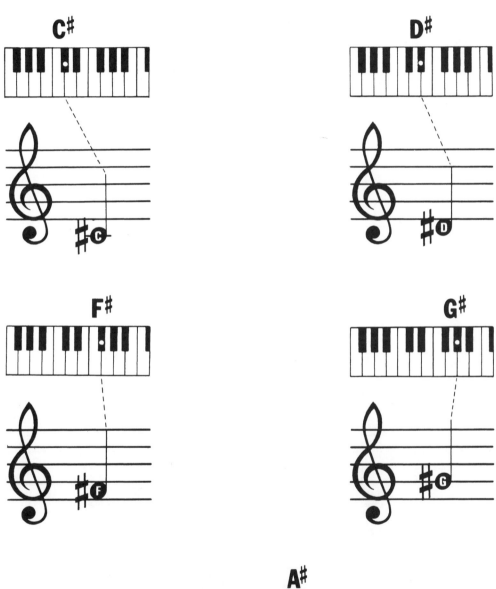

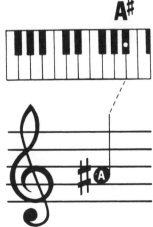

The next song introduces three new chords:

Dm   **E**7   **A**7

I Left My Heart In San Francisco

Words by Douglas Cross
Music by George Cory

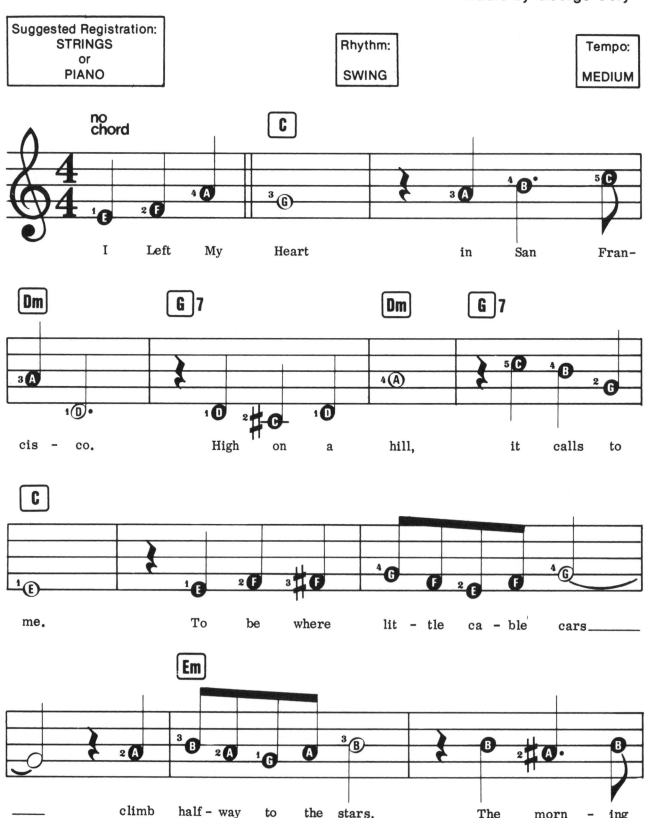

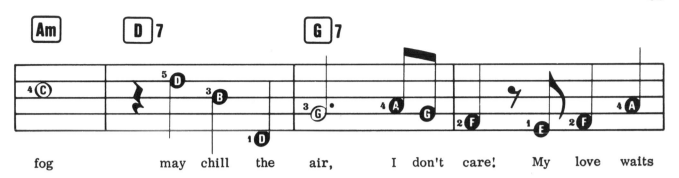

fog   may chill the air,   I don't care! My love waits

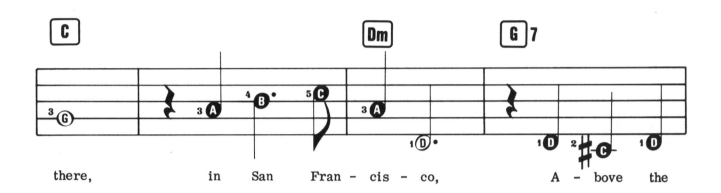

there,   in San Fran - cis - co,   A - bove the

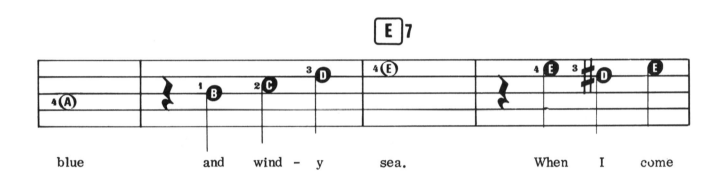

blue   and wind - y sea.   When I come

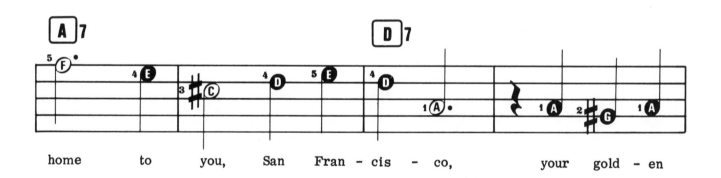

home   to you, San Fran - cis - co,   your gold - en

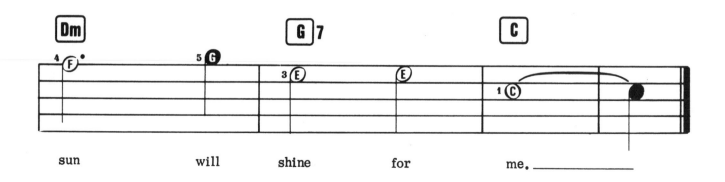

sun   will shine for me. _____

New chords: **Bm** **F#m**

Annie's Song

Words & Music by John Denver

Suggested Registration:
STRINGS
or
PIANO

Rhythm:
WALTZ

Tempo:
MEDIUM

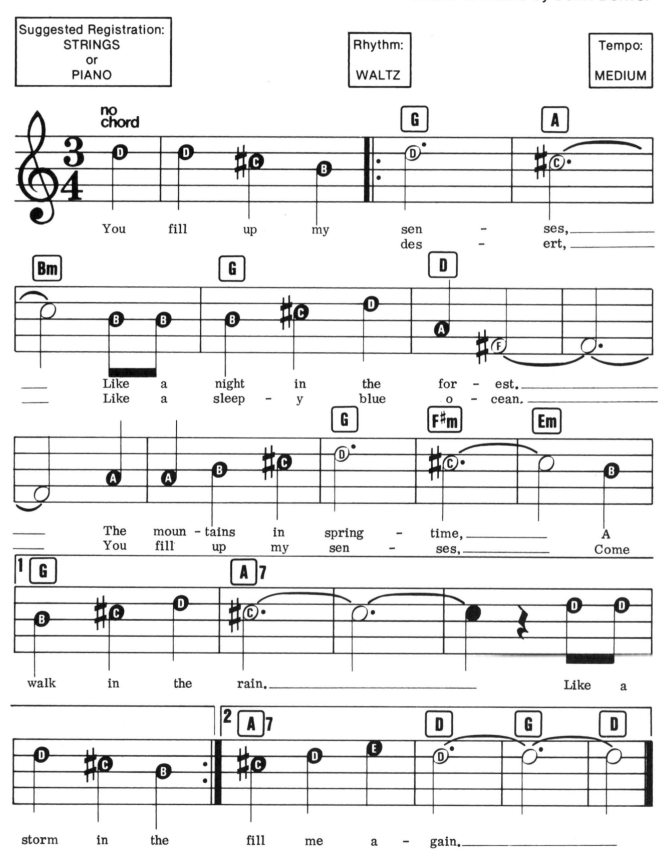

This is the music symbol called the **flat**:

A flat placed before a note tells you to play the *black key* lying immediately to the **left** of the *white key*. This time, the musical pitch becomes **flat**tened:

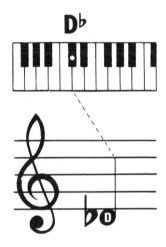

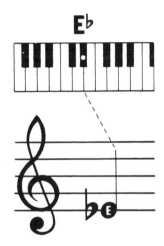

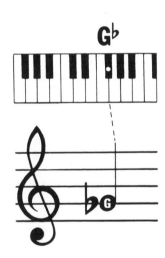

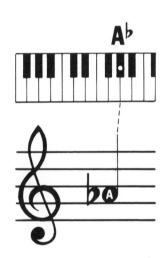

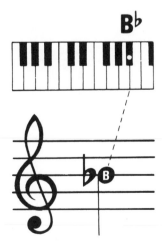

New chords: [E♭] [Cm] [Fm] [B♭]7 [Gm]

Georgia On My Mind

Words by Stuart Gorrell
Music by Hoagy Carmichael

| Suggested Registration: TRUMPET or JAZZ ORGAN | Rhythm: SWING | Tempo: MEDIUM |

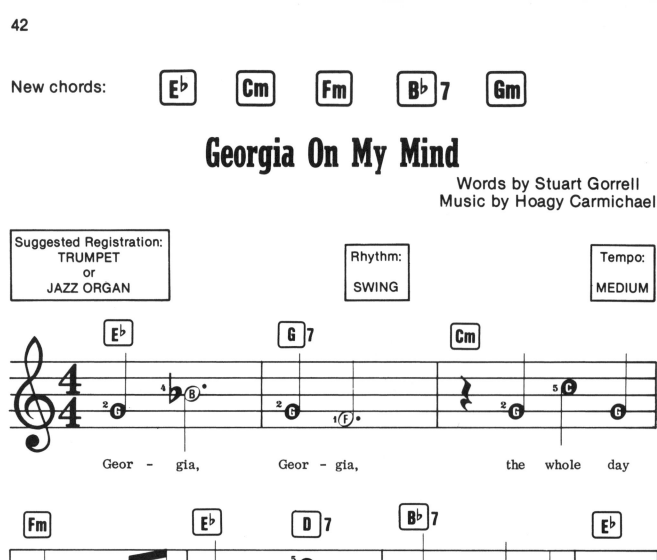

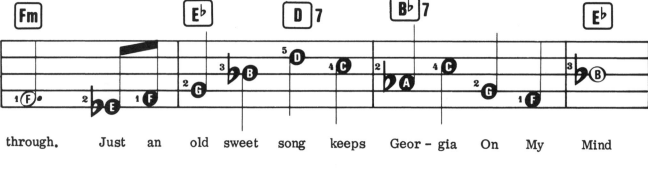

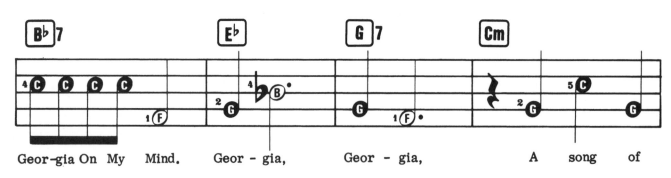

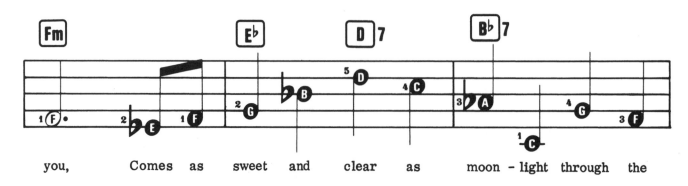

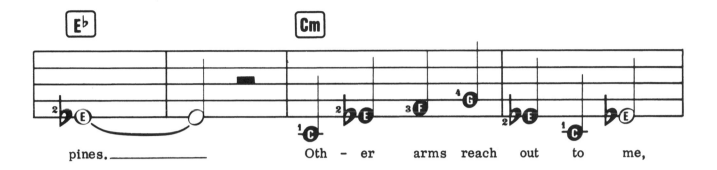

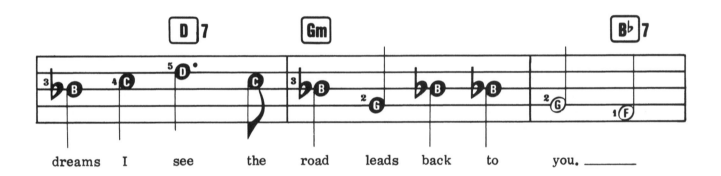

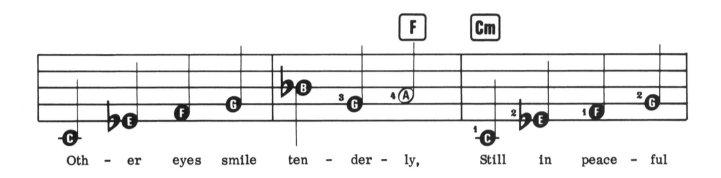

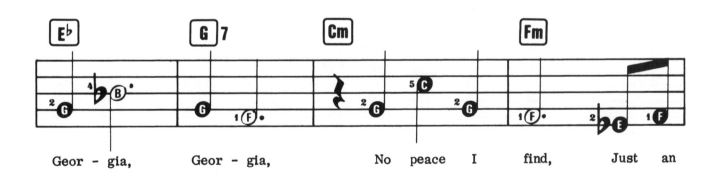

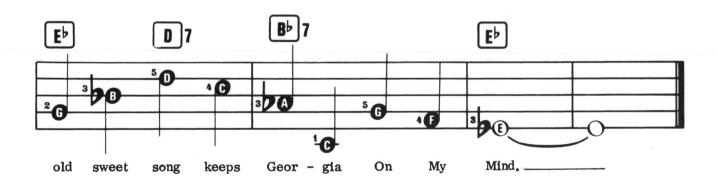

44

Sometimes, a tune will contain both sharps and flats:

Melody Of Love

Music by H. Engelmann

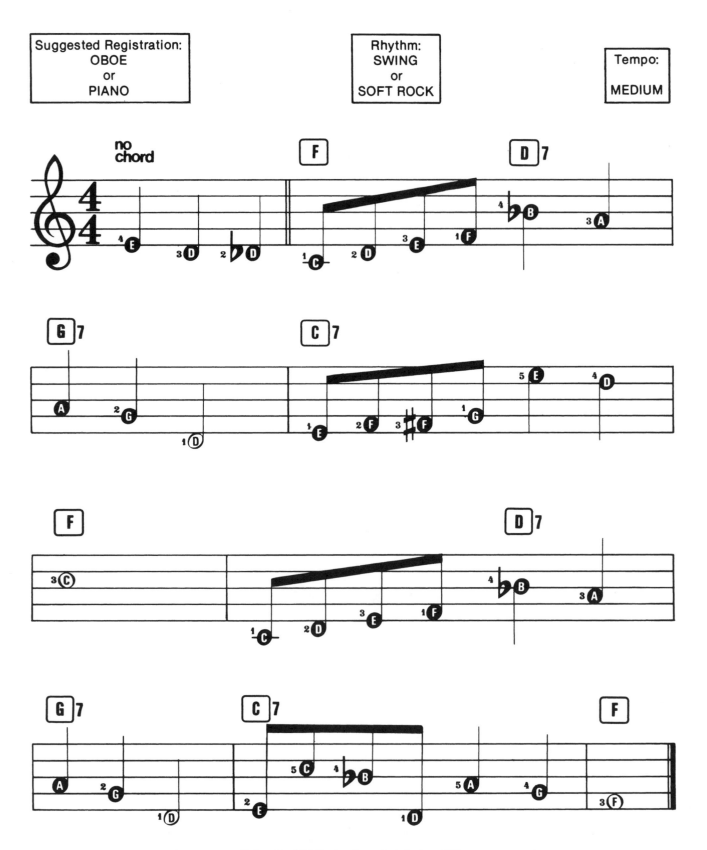

The Triplet. This is a group of *three notes* that are all played in the same amount of time as *two notes* of the same value.

The triplet has a small figure 3 placed either above or below the note group:

QUARTER
NOTE
TRIPLETS ... = ... = ... = **2 beats**

EIGHTH
NOTE
TRIPLETS ... = ... = ... = **1 beat**

The religious ballad "Amazing Grace" has *Eighth Note Triplets* that contrast effectively with pairs of *Eighth Notes* in other measures:

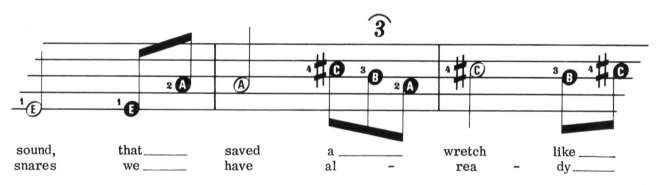

| sound, | that___ | saved | a ___ | wretch | like ___ |
| snares | we ___ | have | al | - | rea | - | dy___ |

The words **D.S. al Fine** appear at the end of the music. This means return to the sign:—

The music is then played through again, and ends at **Fine** in the usual manner.

"Amazing Grace" is an extended arrangement that uses several sharps in the first chorus, followed by a 'lift' in the music pitch for the second chorus. This is known as a **key change**, and flats become a feature of the new key:

Amazing Grace

Traditional

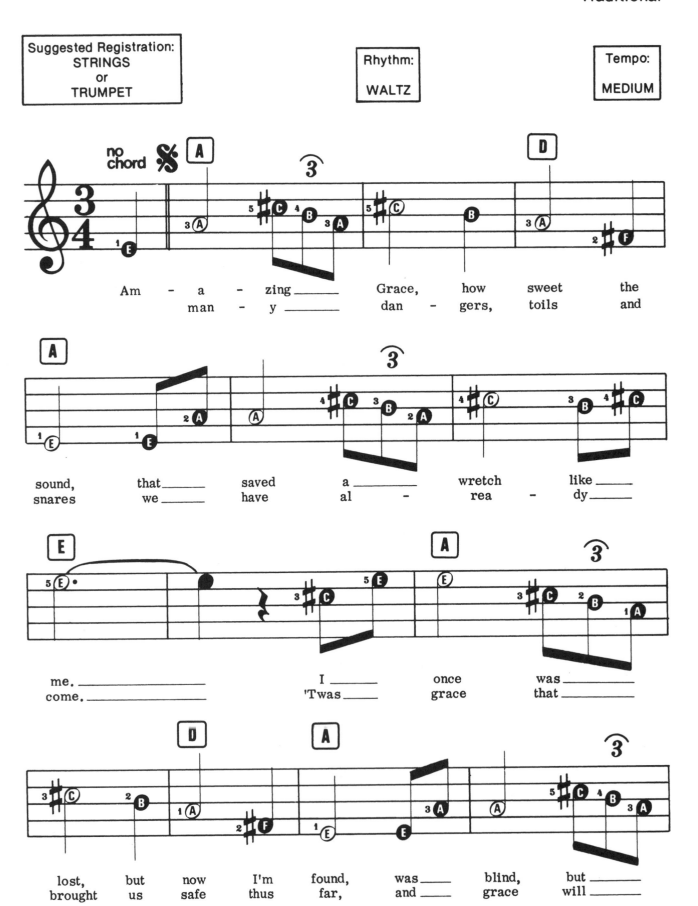

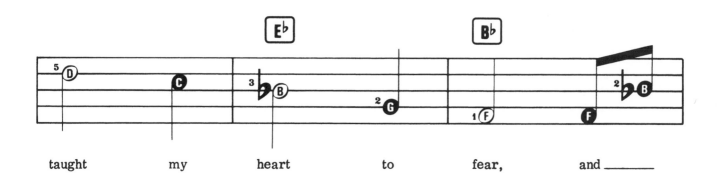

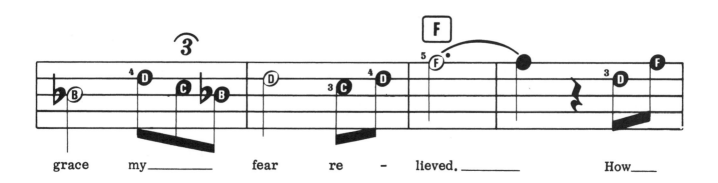

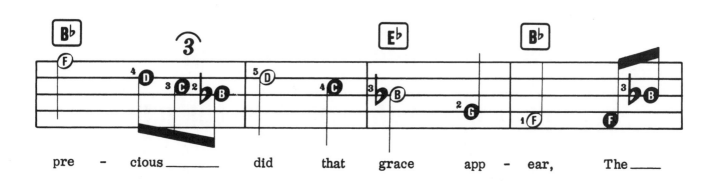

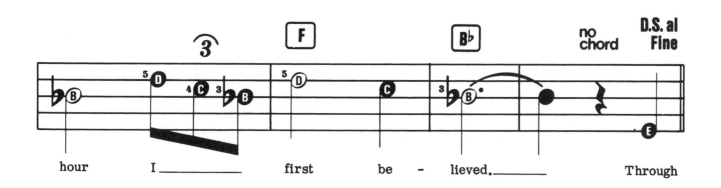

48

Left Hand Fingered Chords. Although Part 1 has centered around the automatic features on your keyboard that provide such effective accompaniment to SFX songs, there is an interesting alternative in using *Left Hand Fingered Chords.* Accompaniment for the melody is made with the left hand playing groups of three or four notes – the chords – in the lower section of your keyboard.

If your keyboard can be switched from 'Automatic' to 'Fingered' accompaniment mode, it is recommended that you learn this type of chord playing.

The step-by-step learning and use of fingered chords in Part 2 will open up exciting new ventures into the world of creative music making through SFX publications.

MASTER CHORD CHART

	MAJOR	MINOR	SEVENTH	MINOR SEVENTH
C	5 2 1	5 2 1	5 3 2 1	5 3 2 1
C♯ D♭	4 2 1	4 2 1	4 3 2 1	4 3 2 1
D	5 3 1	5 2 1	5 3 2 1	5 3 2 1
E♭	5 3 1	5 3 1	5 3 2 1	5 3 2 1
E	4 3 1	5 3 1	4 3 2 1	5 3 2 1
F	5 3 1	5 3 1	5 3 2 1	5 3 2 1
F♯ G♭	4 2 1	4 2 1	5 3 2 1	5 3 2 1
G	5 3 1	5 3 1	5 3 2 1	5 3 2 1
A♭	4 2 1	4 2 1	5 4 2 1	5 4 2 1
A	4 2 1	4 2 1	5 4 2 1	5 4 2 1
B♭	4 2 1	4 2 1	5 4 2 1	5 4 2 1
B	4 2 1	4 2 1	4 3 2 1	4 3 2 1

SFX – SOUNDS 'n' EFFECTS
PART 2

Part 1 of the SFX method showed you how to play popular tunes on your keyboard in a quick and easy way by using the unique SFX letter-note music system and the 'one finger' automatic chord feature.

Part 2 will show you
(1) how to play the professional style 'fingered' chords in your left hand
(2) how to improve and perfect your sight reading and overall playing technique
(3) an easy transition from SFX letter-note music to standard music notation. This is a major step forward in music making that will enable you to play tunes on your keyboard from the immensely popular busker books, and the single note (vocal) lines in everyday sheet music.

Well known melodies have been chosen to help you learn more about music and modern keyboard techniques. Keep exploring all the Sounds 'n' Effects – instrument voices, rhythms, fill ins, tempos, and the add-on effects like vibrato, sustain, reverb, arpeggios, bass accompaniments, sound modulations etc.

Listen to, and play, *all* kinds of music. There are lots of good sounds around!

PL

'Fingered' Chords. The one-finger automatic chord feature on your keyboard enables you to play tunes in a quick and easy way, with a variety of accompaniment effects.

To get the maximum enjoyment and musical benefit from your keyboard, it is recommended you also learn to play all the tunes in the SFX method using 'Fingered' chords. Your Owner's Manual will explain how this feature operates on the keyboard.

The first 15 tunes in SFX-Tutor Part 1 use the chords of C, G, G7 and F; finger positions for left hand are illustrated below. Practise these four basic chords, keeping your wrist just above keyboard level and fingers slightly curved onto each of the notes to be played. The fingering numbers are a general guide only, as you may find it easier to use different fingering between more rapid chord changes later.

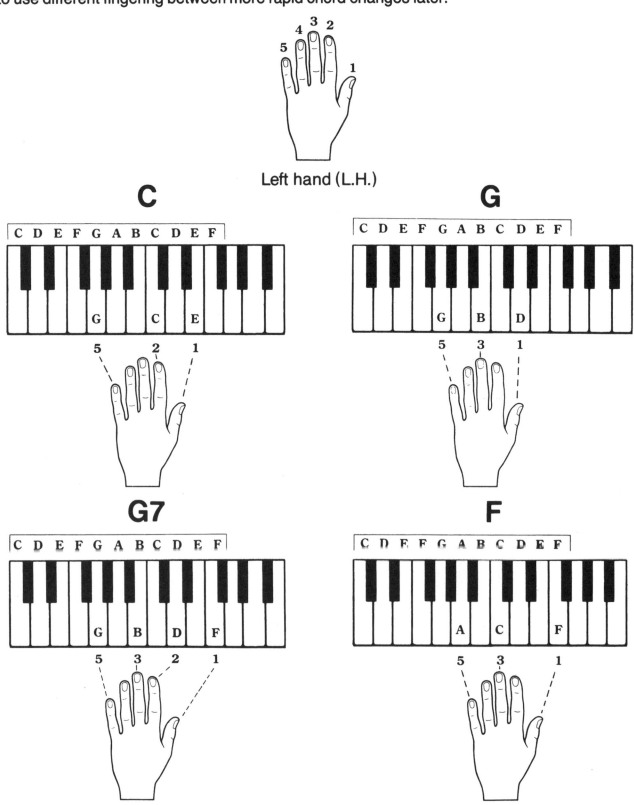

The following 'fingered' chords can be used to play the remaining tunes in
SFX-Tutor Part 1.

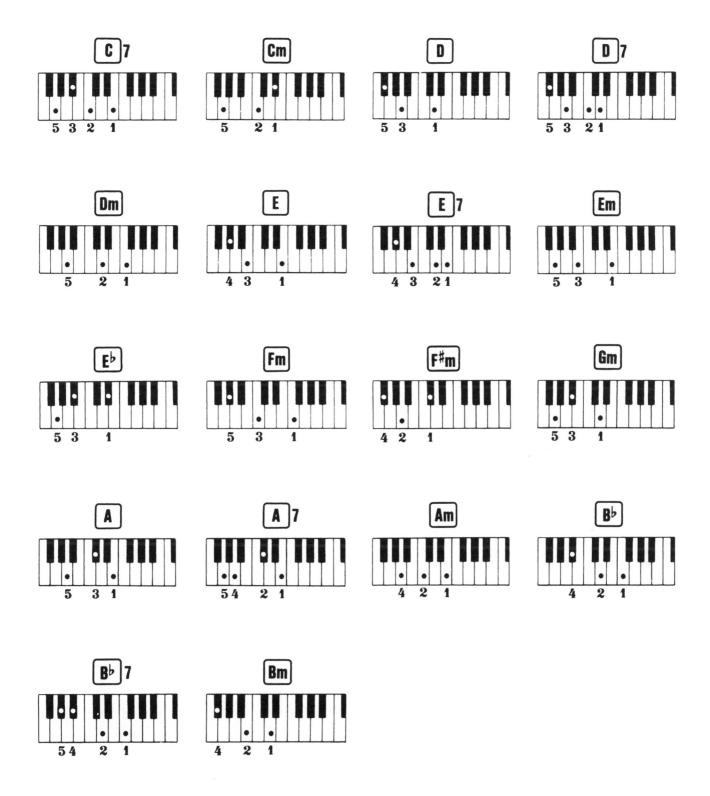

The well known tunes you are about to play will introduce new 'fingered' chords. Learn
them, and you will soon be familiar with their sequences in popular music.

A useful 3-point practice routine: (1) play the melody on its own with the right hand,
(2) repeat several times using the 'one finger' automatic chord accompaniment, and
finally (3) play the song using 'fingered' chords.

By following this routine, and using the variety of Sounds 'n' Effects on your keyboard,
you will become a competent and creative player.

The Quarter Note Triplet: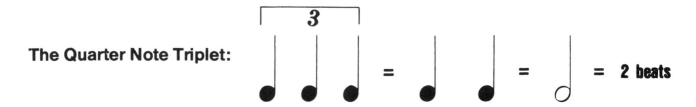

Quarter note triplets are very popular in slow ballads. This song from The Pyjama Game makes effective use of these 'laid back' phrases.

New chords:

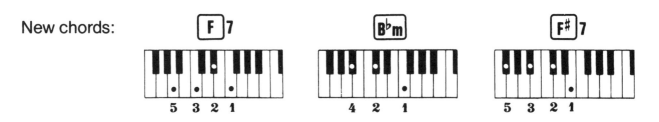

Hey There

Words & Music by
Richard Adler & Jerry Ross

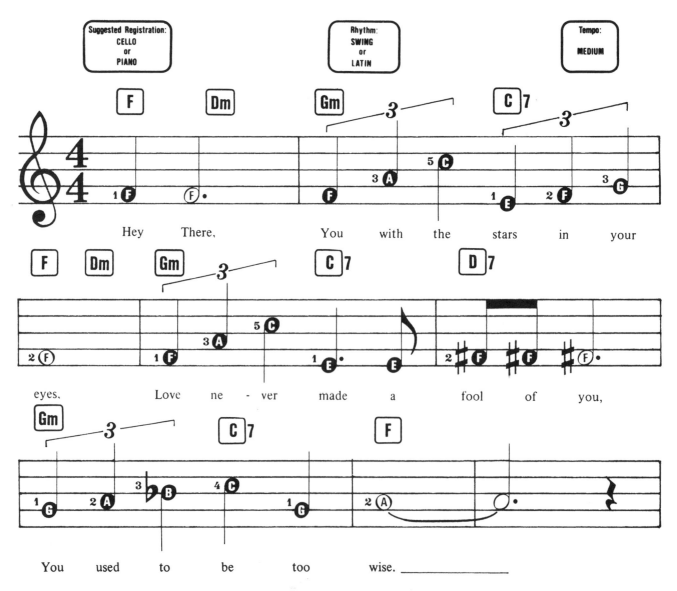

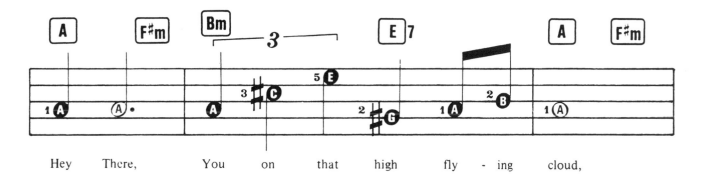

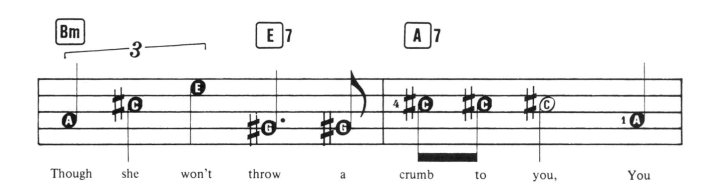

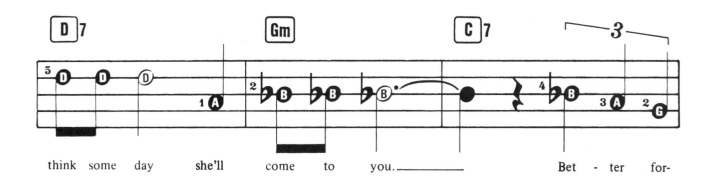

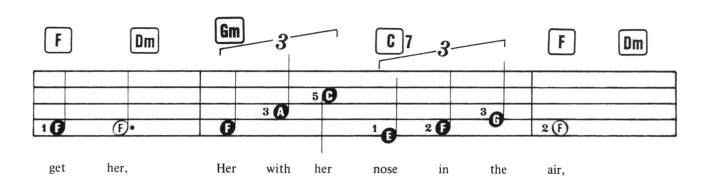

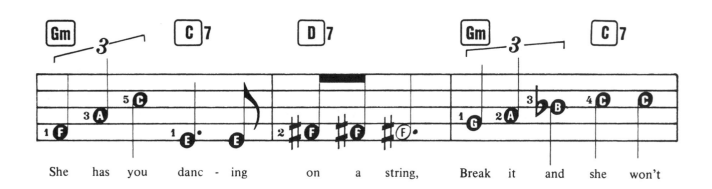

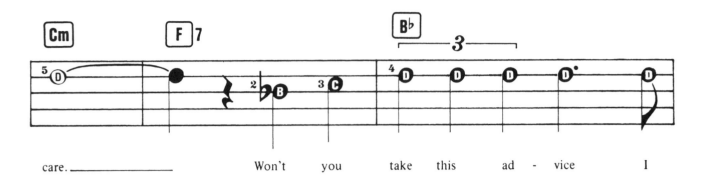

care._____ Won't you take this ad - vice I

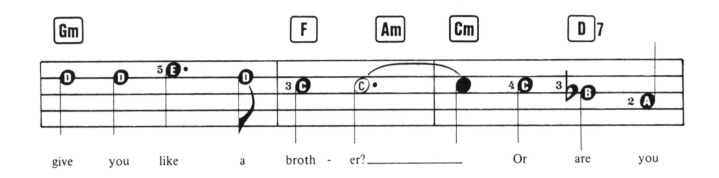

give you like a broth - er?_____ Or are you

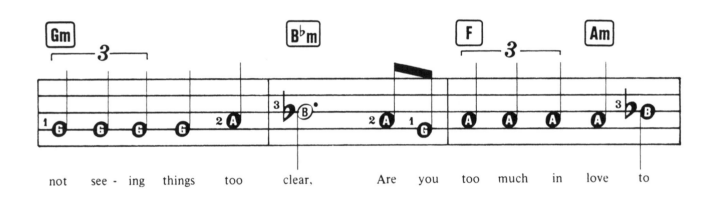

not see - ing things too clear, Are you too much in love to

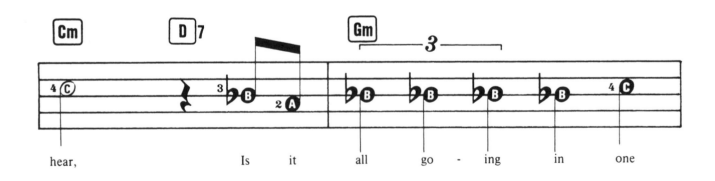

hear, Is it all go - ing in one

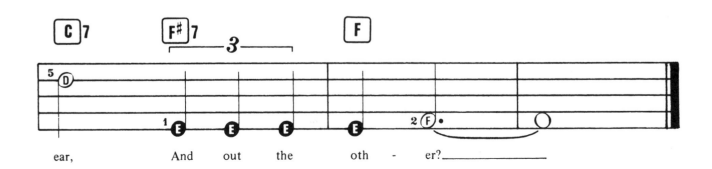

ear, And out the oth - er?_____

The next song has two separate Repeat sections. The latter (pages 10-11) has a combined 1st and 2nd time bracket, with the 3rd time bracket providing the final chord and melody note.

Feelings
(Dime)

English Words & Music by Morris Albert
Spanish Lyric by Thomas Fundora

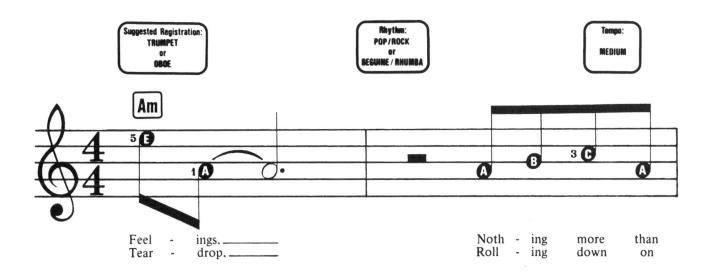

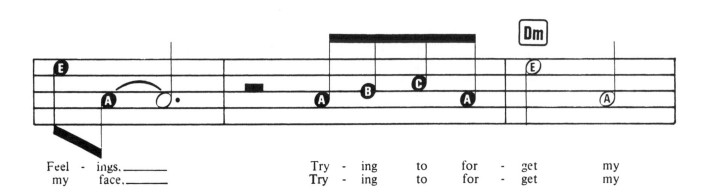

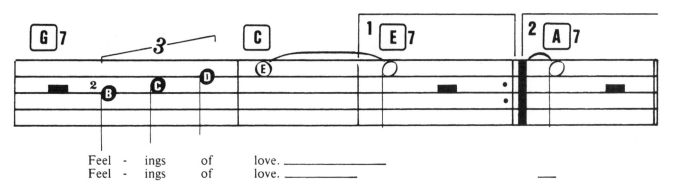

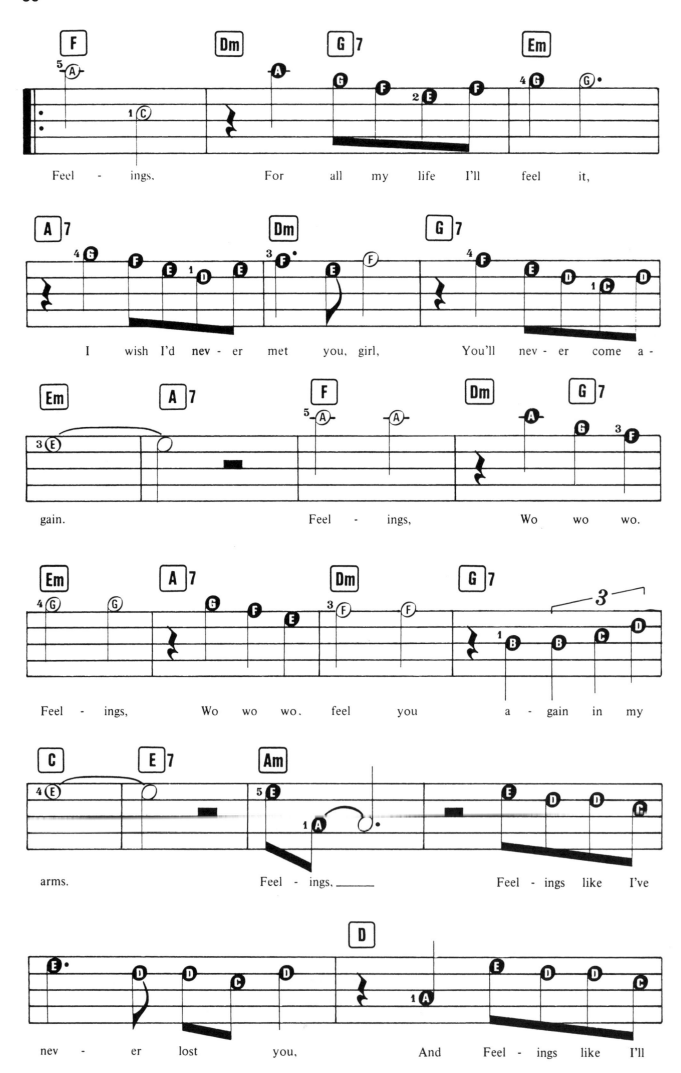

nev - er have you ... a - gain in my

heart. _____ heart. _____

The Sixteenth Note has two tails:

In pairs, and groups of four, the
tails become parallel beams:

The Sixteenth Note has a time value that
is one-half of an Eighth Note. A pair of
Sixteenth Notes therefore equals one
Eighth Note:

The following three measures each show how notes of similar value appear in
$\frac{4}{4}$ time. Play the sequence through at a steady tempo, following the counting guide
below each note.

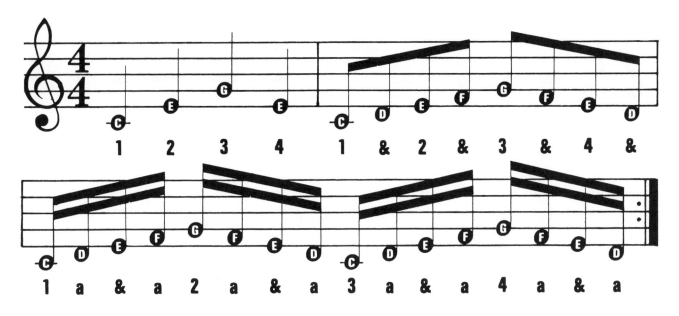

Sixteenth notes are frequently beamed to dotted eighth notes. This follows the rule that a dot after a note increases its value by one-half:

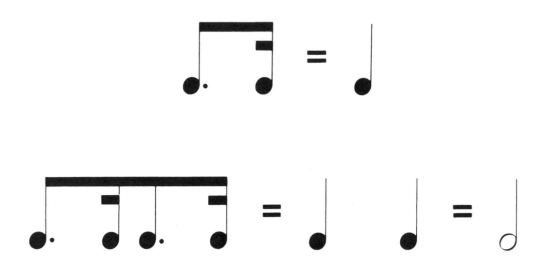

It is the little extra time value, and resulting natural stress on each dotted note, that gives the bouncy 'lilt' to many songs like the ever popular Beatles hit "Yellow Submarine".

Yellow Submarine

Words & Music by
John Lennon & Paul McCartney

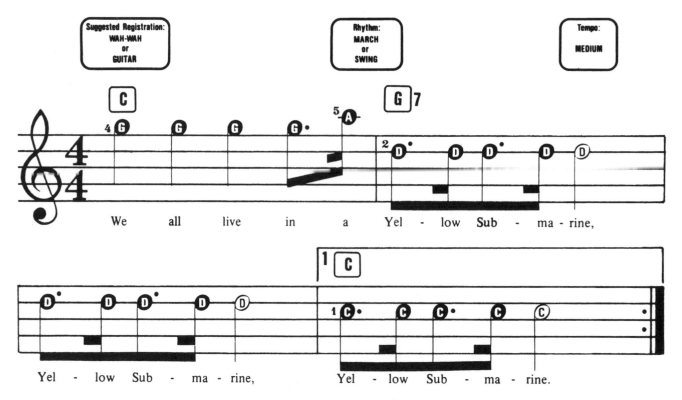

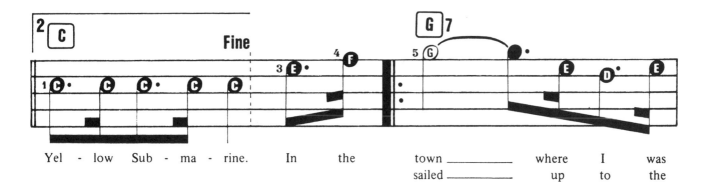

Yel - low Sub - ma - rine. In the town ———— where I was

sailed ———— up to the

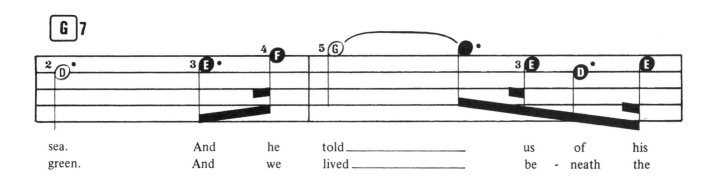

born, Lived a man ———— who sailed the

sun, Till we found ———— the **sea** of

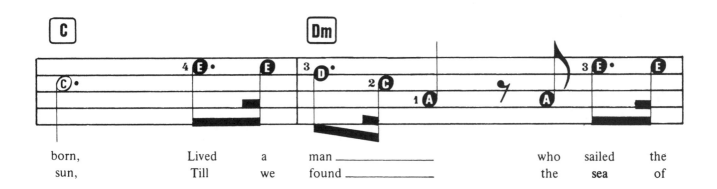

sea. And he told ———— us of his

green. And we lived ———— be - neath the

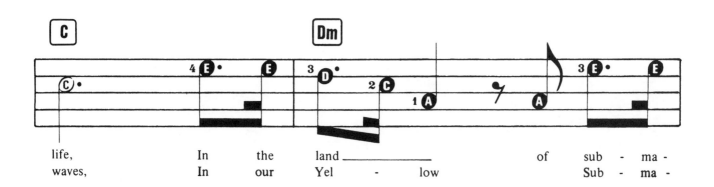

life, In the land ———— of sub - ma -

waves, In our Yel - low Sub - ma -

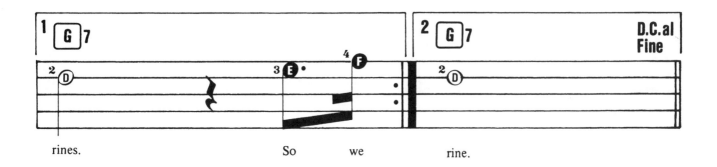

rines. So we

rine.

Toreador Song has both eighth note, and dotted eighth note/sixteenth note patterns. Played correctly, these contrasting rhythmic phrases add extra spirit to this famous tune.

Toreador Song
(From "Carmen")

By Georges Bizet

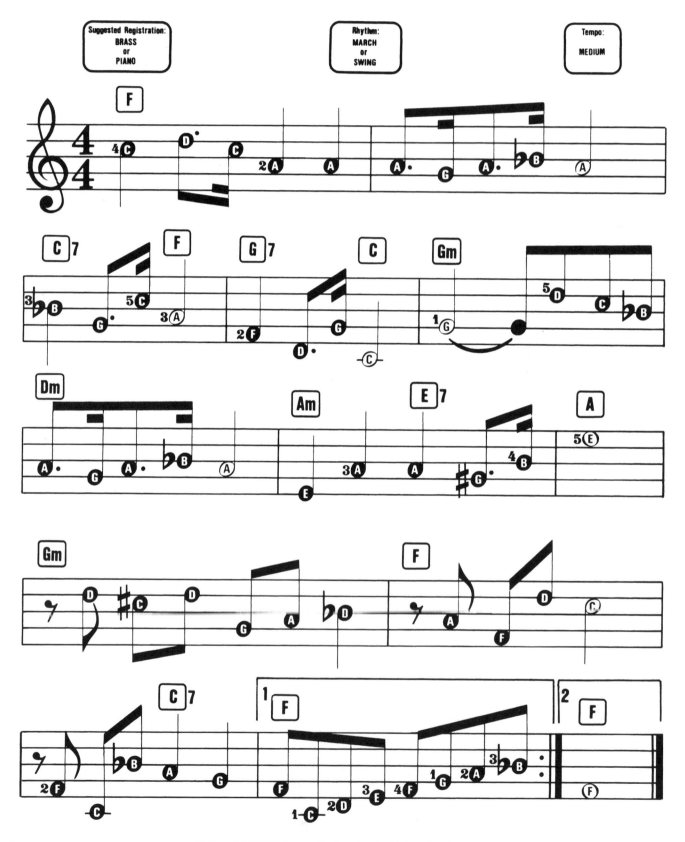

The slow ballad "When Sunny Gets Blue" has a variety of sixteenth note figures.

Firstly, the frequently used dotted eighth note/sixteenth note phrase:

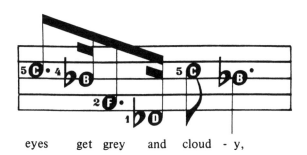

eyes   get grey   and   cloud - y,

The fourth beat of the following measure has the less common reversed form where the first note ("pat-") is quickly followed by the longer sounding second note ("-ter"):

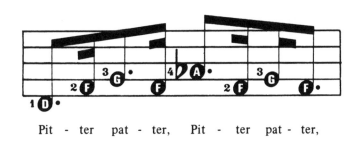

Pit - ter   pat - ter,   Pit - ter   pat - ter,

The seventh measure of the song has a pair of sixteenth notes following the dotted quarter note:

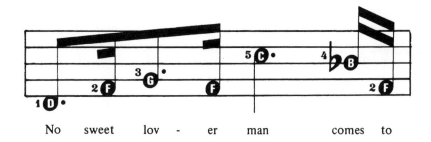

No   sweet   lov - er   man   comes to

Play each of the above song fragments in slow, strict tempo. You will soon get to recognise such phrases and be able to play them correctly in all kinds of music.

New chords:

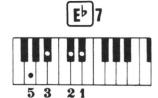  

When Sunny Gets Blue

Words by Jack Segal
Music by Marvin Fisher

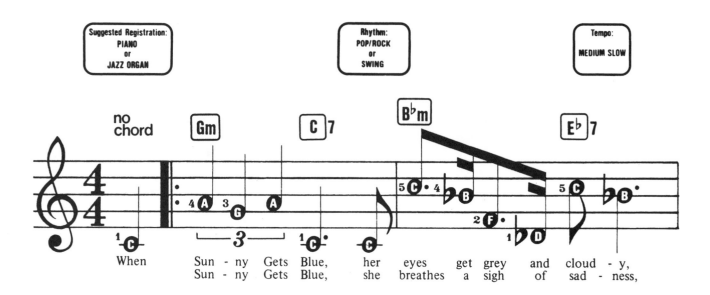

When Sun - ny Gets Blue, her eyes get grey and cloud - y,
Sun - ny Gets Blue, she breathes a sigh of sad - ness,

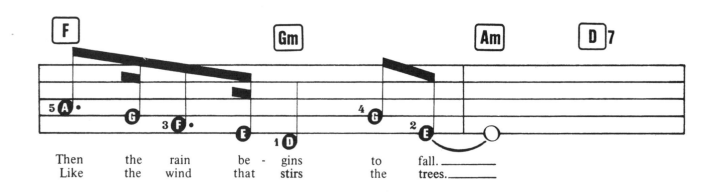

Then the rain be - gins to fall.
Like the wind that stirs to the trees.

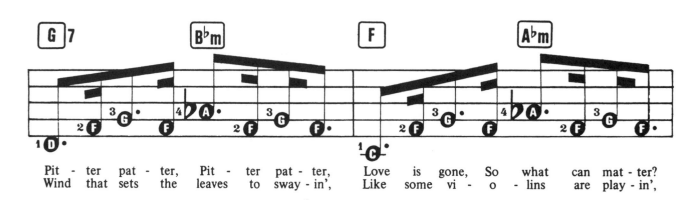

Pit - ter pat - ter, Pit - ter pat - ter, Love is gone, So what can mat - ter?
Wind that sets the leaves to sway - in', Like some vi - o - lins are play - in',

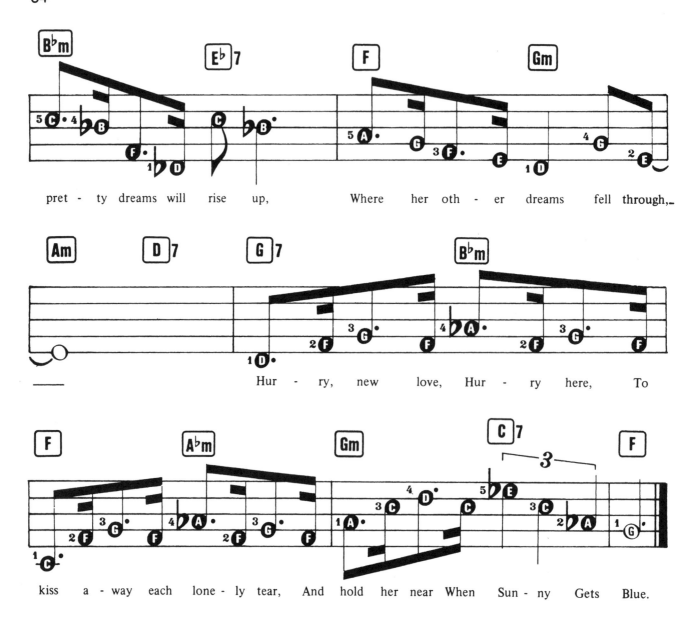

pret - ty dreams will rise up, Where her oth - er dreams fell through,___

___ Hur - ry, new love, Hur - ry here, To

kiss a - way each lone - ly tear, And hold her near When Sun - ny Gets Blue.

Tunes may often go below Middle C, and others extend above top A. Further leger lines are used for these notes.

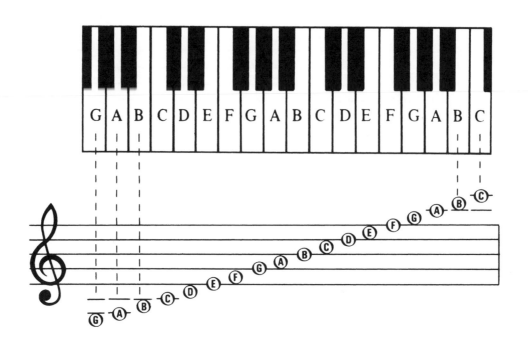

The next two pieces, "Little April Shower", and "In The Hall Of The Mountain King", use these new notes, and also introduce a musical punctuation sign called the **staccato**.

The staccato is a dot placed over ⌐ or under ↓ a note, indicating that it should be shortened and detached from the following note. Its time value remains unchanged.

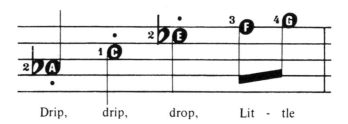

Both tunes have a **Coda**, an Italian word meaning 'tail'. The Coda is a separated section of music that forms the end of an arrangement, and is represented by the sign ⊕ .

Da Capo al Coda, usually abbreviated to **D.C. al Coda**, means return to the very beginning (da capo) of the music, and play through again until you reach the term and sign al Coda ⊕ just above the stave. From this point you make a skip to the Coda and play to the end of the music.

New chords:

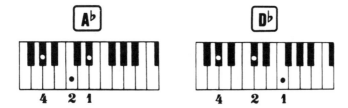

Little April Shower

Words by Larry Morey
Music by Frank Churchill

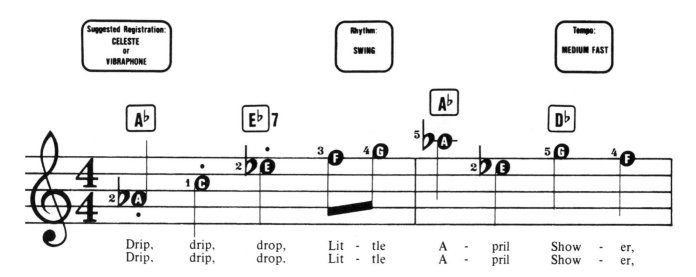

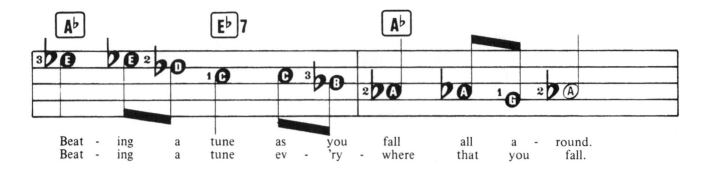

Beat - ing a tune as you fall all a - round.
Beat - ing a tune ev - 'ry - where that you fall.

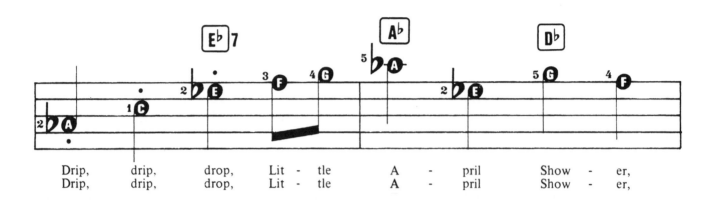

Drip, drip, drop, Lit - tle A - pril Show - er,
Drip, drip, drop, Lit - tle A - pril Show - er,

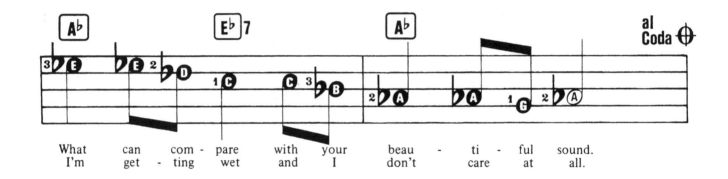

What can com - pare with your beau - ti - ful sound.
I'm get - ting wet and I don't care at all.

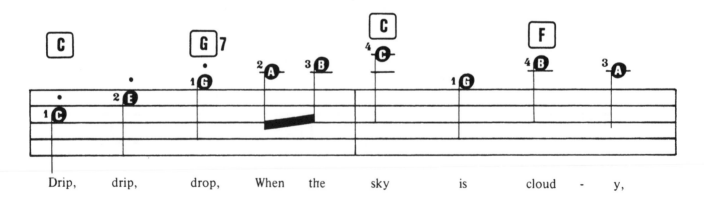

Drip, drip, drop, When the sky is cloud - y,

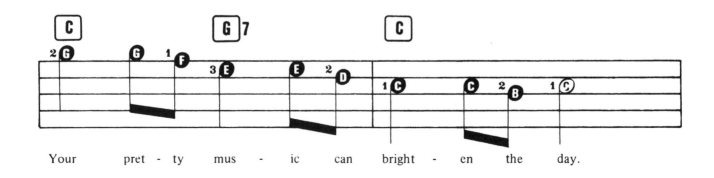

Your pret - ty mus - ic can bright - en the day.

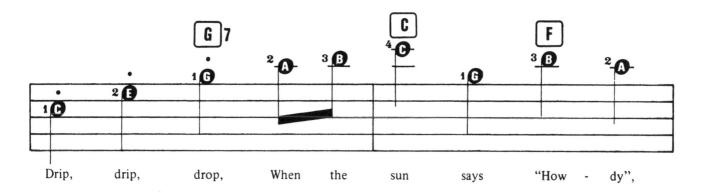

Drip, drip, drop, When the sun says "How - dy",

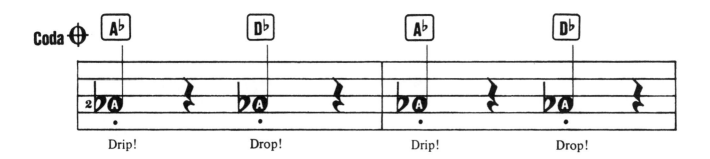

You say "Good - bye" right a - way._____

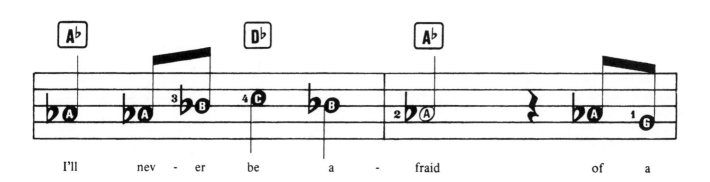

Coda

Drip!   Drop!   Drip!   Drop!

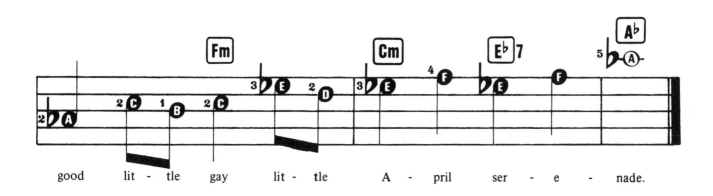

I'll   nev - er   be   a -   fraid   of   a

good   lit - tle   gay   lit - tle   A - pril   ser - e - nade.

Attention to correct fingering is essential in this popular classical tune. Set the Tempo at 'Medium Slow' until you can perform the cross-over fingerings smoothly.

In The Hall Of The Mountain King
(From "Peer Gynt")

By Edvard Grieg

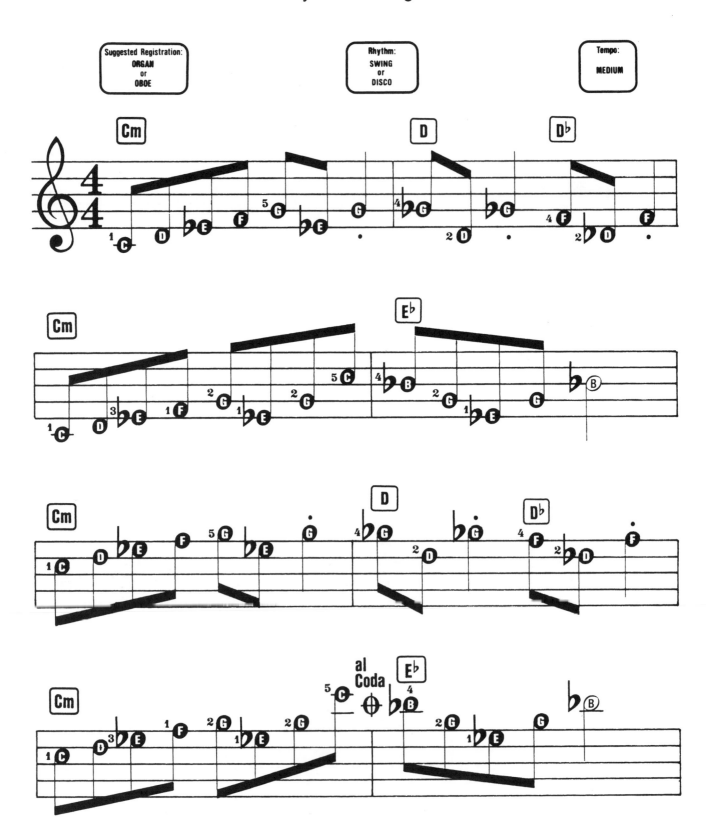

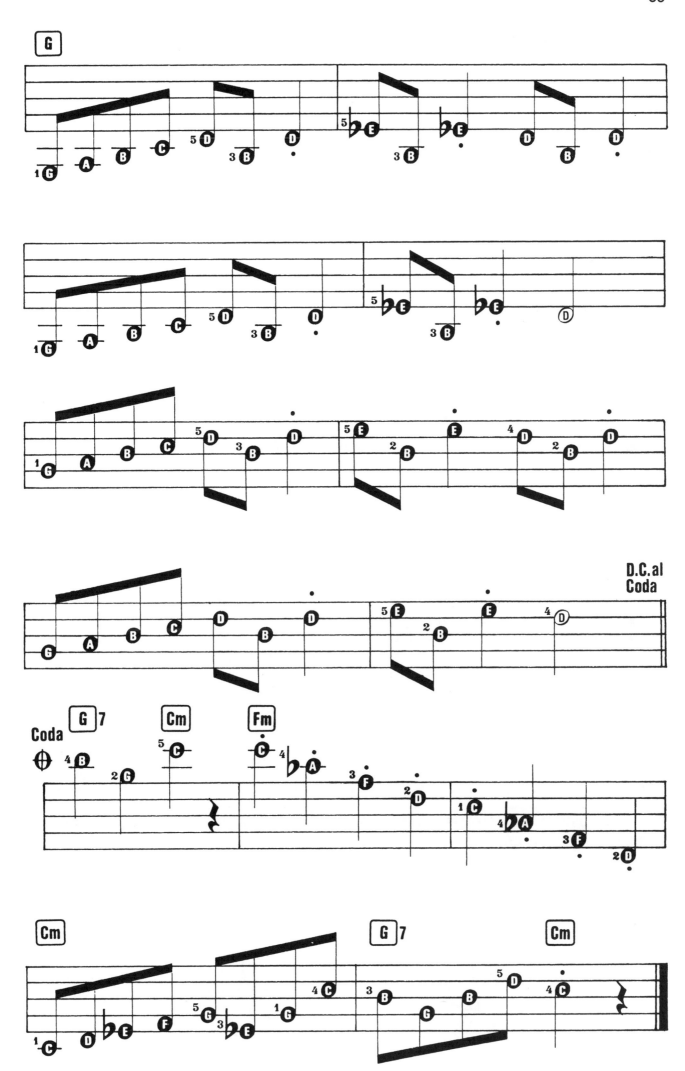

A slur is a curved line which spans notes of differing pitch, indicating they are to be played in a smooth unbroken manner:

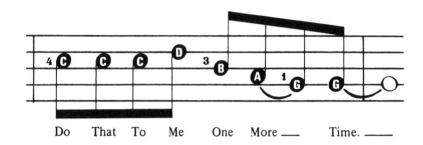

In songs, the lyrics often dictate where a slur is required. The word "More" is a blend of two notes, to be sung *and* played smoothly.

A slur will often cover a series of notes, forming a smooth phrase:

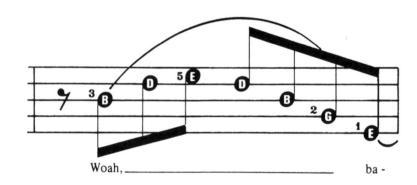

"Do That To Me One More Time" has 𝐂 for the time signature. This denotes Common Time, and is simply another way of writing $\frac{4}{4}$ time.

Do That To Me One More Time

Words & Music by
Toni Tennille

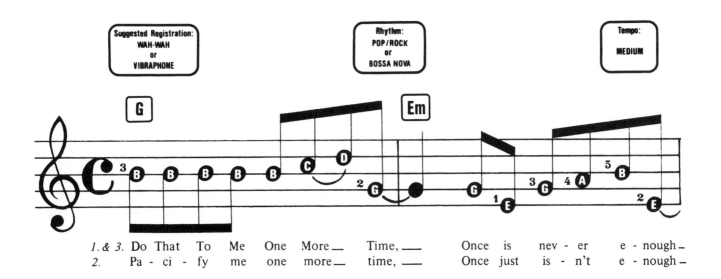

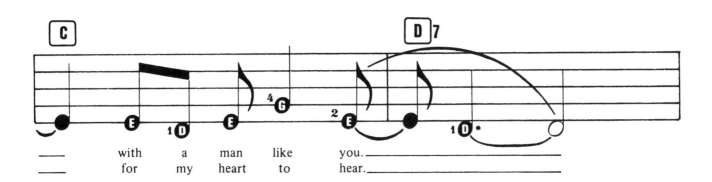

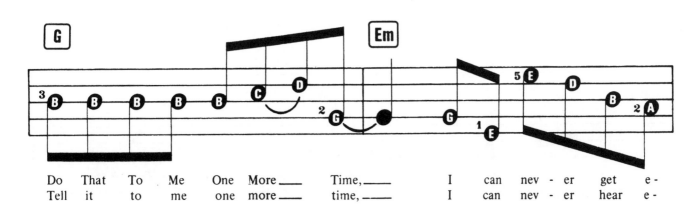

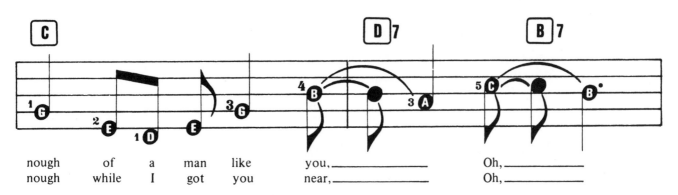

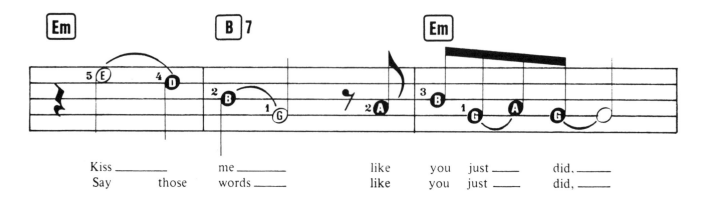

Kiss _____ me _____ like you just ____ did, ____
Say those words _____ like you just ____ did, ____

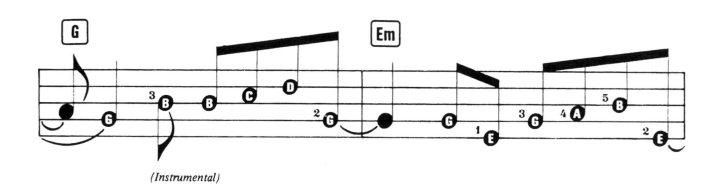

Oh ba - by, ____ Do that to me once a - gain.
Oh ba - by, ____ Tell it to me once a - gain.

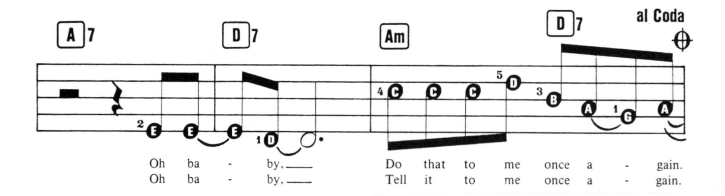

(Instrumental)

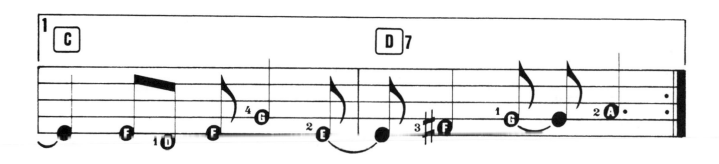

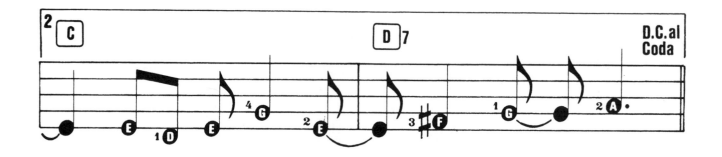

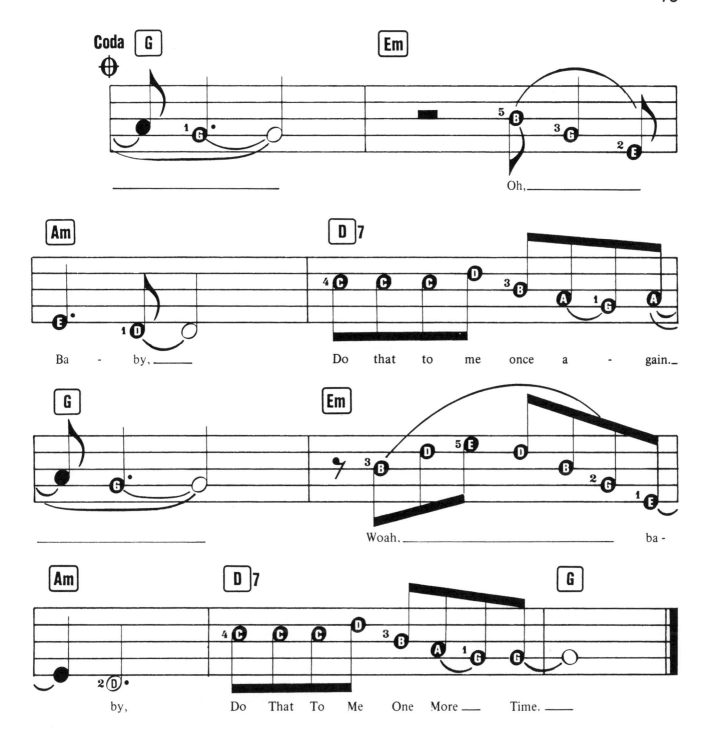

The automatic features of the modern keyboard can be used effectively at the beginning and during the performance of a song to add variety and character.

The introduction to "We've Only Just Begun" can be played melody only, with no rhythm or chord accompaniment. Rhythm, set at 'Medium Slow', is put on 'Key Start'. The first chord you play following the introduction will start the rhythm accompaniment.

The 'Select' button in the 'Tone Section' is a quick and easy way to change voice registration. The instrument sounds have been paired so that depressing the 'Select' button while playing gives a suitable voice contrast.

An effective ending can be made by turning the Rhythm off where indicated in the penultimate measure and playing the last phrase at a decreasing tempo.

The final measure has a Fermata ⌢ indicating that the last note can be sustained at will.

We've Only Just Begun

Words by Paul Williams
Music by Roger Nichols

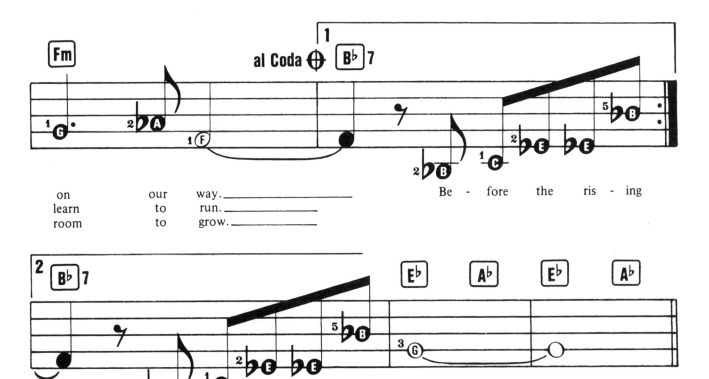

on our way._____
learn to run._____
room to grow._____

Be - fore the ris - ing

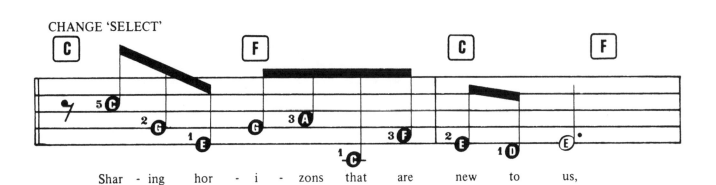

_____ And yes, We've just be - gun._____

CHANGE 'SELECT'

Shar - ing hor - i - zons that are new to us,

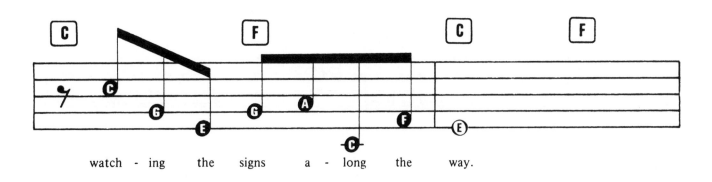

watch - ing the signs a - long the way.

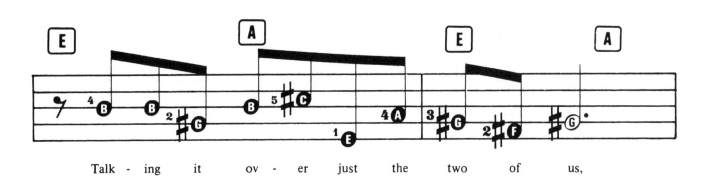

Talk - ing it ov - er just the two of us,

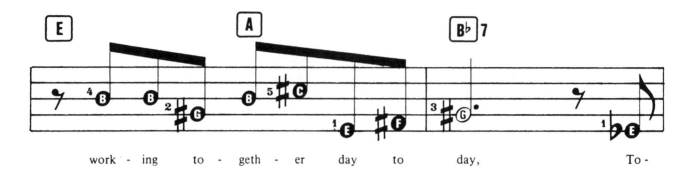

work - ing to - geth - er day to day, To -

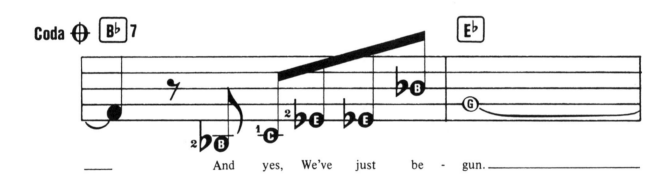

CHANGE 'SELECT'

D.S. al Coda

geth - er, To - geth - er._____ And when the eve - ning

Coda

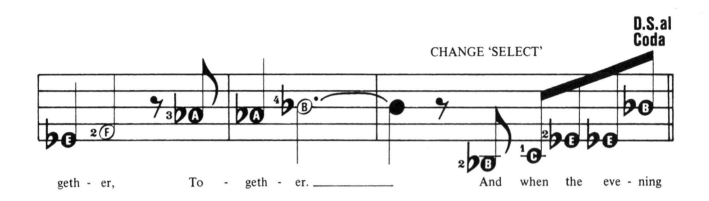

_____ And yes, We've just be - gun._____

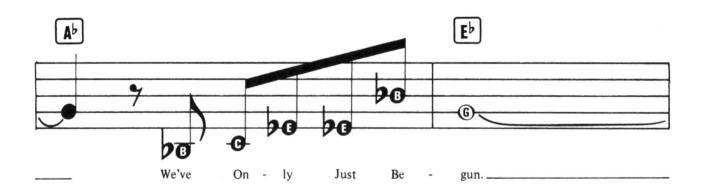

_____ We've On - ly Just Be - gun._____

'RHYTHM' OFF

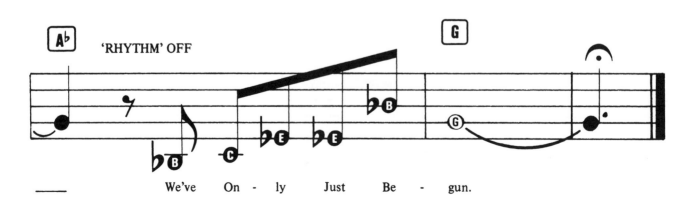

_____ We've On - ly Just Be - gun.

So far your keyboard playing has made good progress using SFX music with its letter-note identification.

'Fingered' chords have extended your playing expertise together with a working knowledge of basic harmony in left hand chord structuring.

You are now ready to play from standard music notation!

This is another major step forward that will provide new creative dimensions to keyboard playing.

Note names for the five lines and four spaces of the staff can be easily remembered by mnemonics:

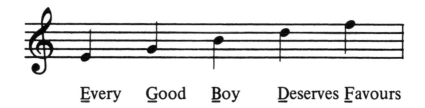

E̲very   G̲ood   B̲oy   D̲eserves F̲avours

F̲   A̲   C̲   E̲

Notes below and above the staff have the same mnemonic:

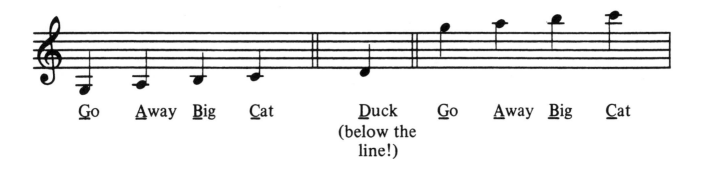

G̲o   A̲way   B̲ig   C̲at   D̲uck   G̲o   A̲way   B̲ig   C̲at
                              (below the
                               line!)

The waltz "Kiss Me Again" by Victor Herbert introduces standard music notation at the 16th measure.

Kiss Me Again

By Victor Herbert

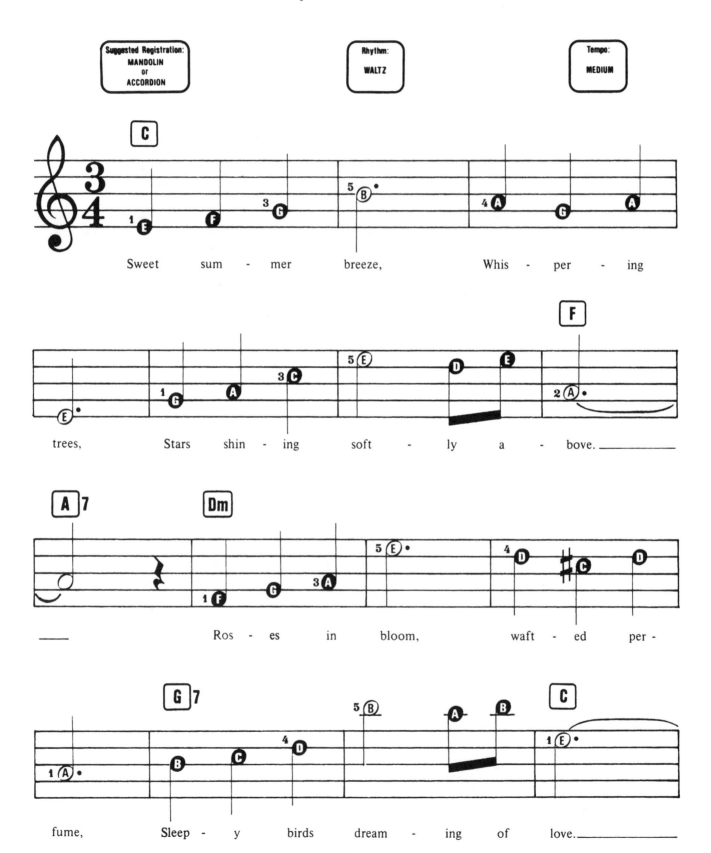

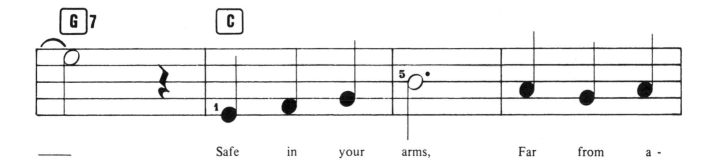

Safe in your arms, Far from a-

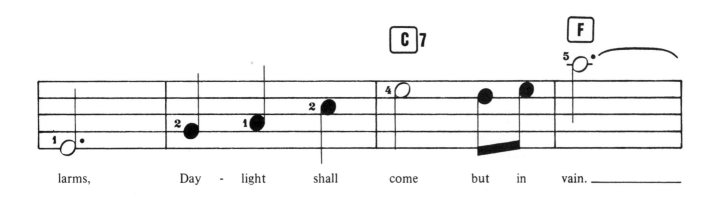

larms, Day - light shall come but in vain. _____

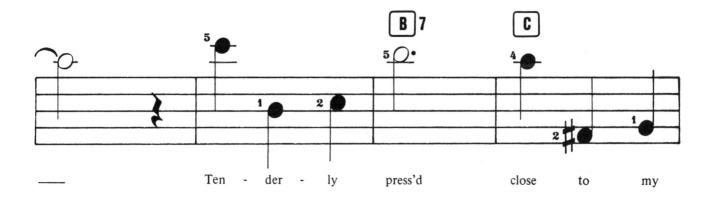

_____ Ten - der - ly press'd close to my

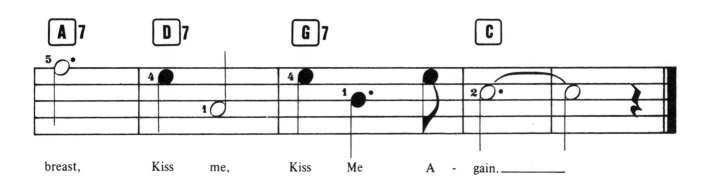

breast, Kiss me, Kiss Me A - gain. _____

"Adios Muchachos" is the ideal tune to play in Tango rhythm.

SFX letter-notes are written for the first eight measures, followed by standard music notation for the melodic repeat and finale.

Keep the tempo moderately slow to begin with, and practise up to a lively tango pace.

Adios Muchachos

Traditional

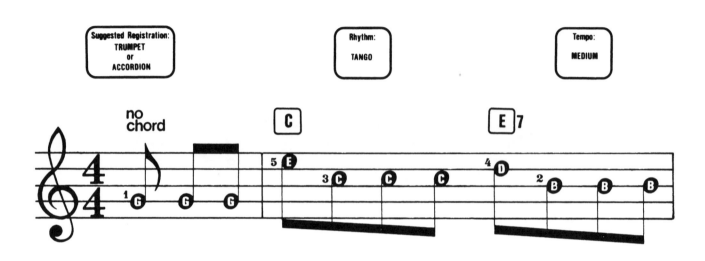

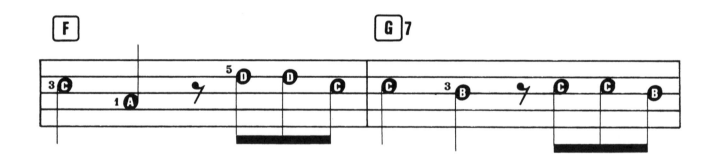

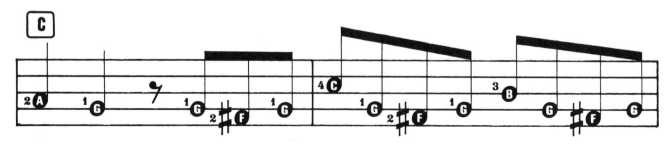

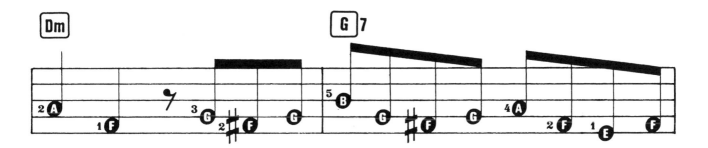

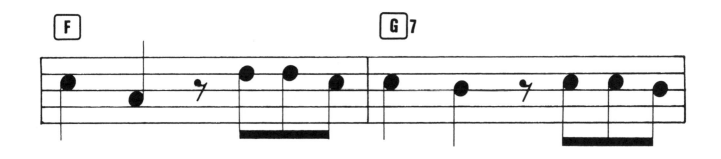

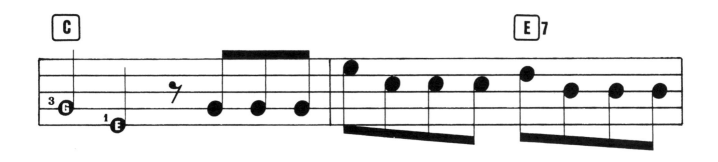

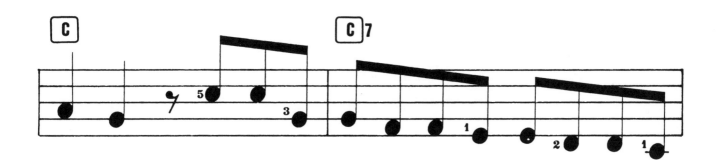

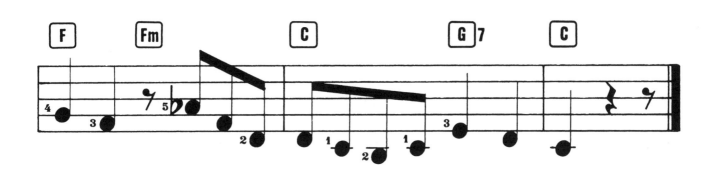

Music is often written in Cut Common Time, with the time signature:

This is $\frac{2}{2}$ time, giving a two-to-the-measure feel in the music. Instead of the quarter note representing one beat (as in Common Time, $\frac{4}{4}$), in Cut Common Time the beat becomes a half note. As a result, the music sounds twice as fast as it appears. This is simply illustrated using the lyrics and music of "Ob-La-Di, Ob-La-Da".

In Common Time, with four steady beats to the measure, the song is far too slow:

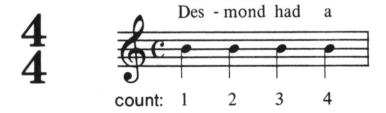

In Cut Common Time however, with two half notes to the measure and each half note having one beat

the song will flow at a much more lively pace, and the rhythm will feel right:

When playing in Cut Common Time it is best to avoid complex Rhythm and Bass accompaniments in songs with frequent chord changes.

Ob-La-Di, Ob-La-Da

Words & Music by
John Lennon & Paul McCartney

84

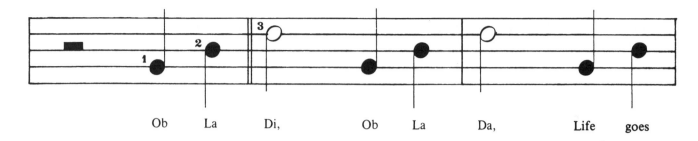

Ob La Di, Ob La Da, Life goes

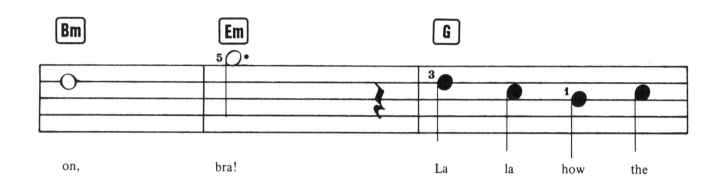

on, bra! La la how the

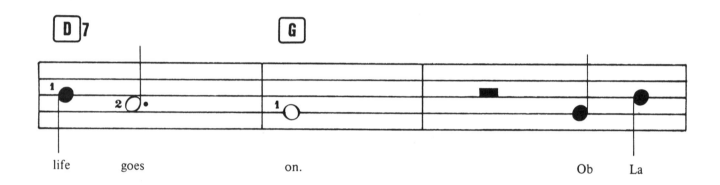

life goes on. Ob La

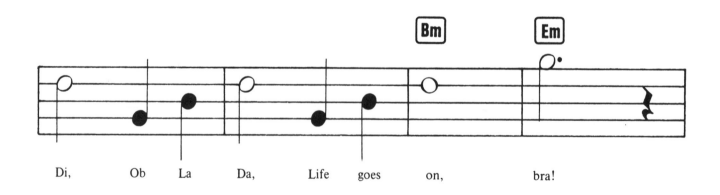

Di, Ob La Da, Life goes on, bra!

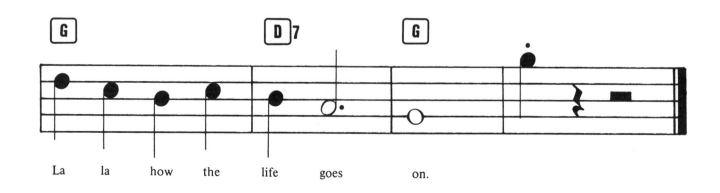

La la how the life goes on.

Sometimes a song will have a $\frac{2}{4}$ time signature, being two quarter notes to the measure. It is a popular time signature for marches, and lively show tunes like "Diamonds Are A Girl's Best Friend".

Diamonds Are A Girl's Best Friend

Words by Leo Robin
Music by Jule Styne

Key Signatures and Accidentals. A scale is a series of adjacent notes. This is the scale of C:

Only the white notes on your keyboard are used to play the scale of C.

If a scale starts on the note of F, it is necessary to play a B♭ in that scale:

As the note B♭ features throughout the scale of F, a **key signature** can be written at the beginning of the staff:

This is called the key signature of F, and it is then no longer necessary to place a flat sign before the note B in the scale:

The key signature of F indicates that every note B is flattened, irrespective of its position in or around the staff:

The song "Uptown Girl" is in the key of F. A number of notes in the middle section have flats written before them. These are called **accidentals**.

An accidental in a measure will apply to that particular note for the remainder of the measure:

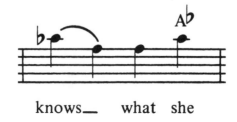

knows_ what she

Subsequent measures are not affected by an accidental; the notes revert back to their basic form:

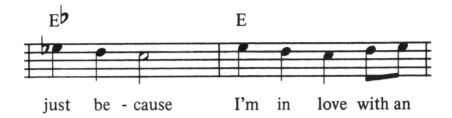

just be - cause   I'm in love with an

Sometimes a natural sign ♮ may be used as a reminder:

just be - cause   I'm in love with an

A scale starting on the note G requires an F♯:

A key signature of G, with the F♯ as illustrated below, will govern that note throughout the music:

The second song "So Nice", is in the key of G. In the first measure, a natural is used to cancel the F♯. This natural is an accidental, and the key signature's F♯ again takes effect in the subsequent measure:

Some-one to   hold me tight,   that would be ver - y nice,

Remember: accidentals, whether sharps, flats, or naturals, alter the adjacent note and its recurrence within the measure only:

Should it be you and me,   I could see   it would be   nice.

New chords: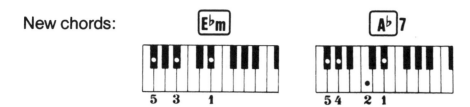

Uptown Girl

Words & Music by
Billy Joel

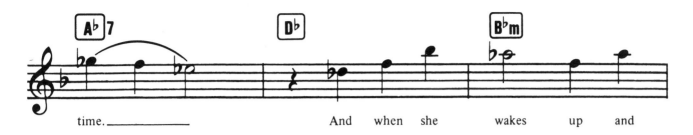

time._____ And when she wakes up and

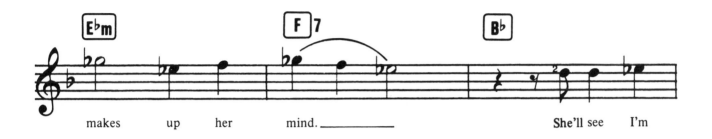

makes up her mind._____ **She'll** see I'm

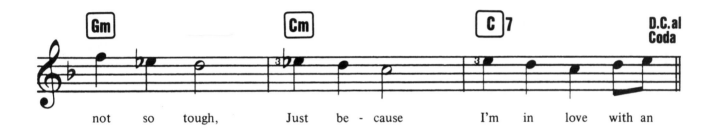

not so tough, Just be - cause I'm in love with an

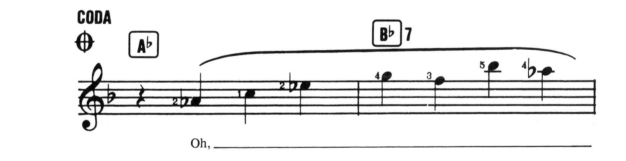

Oh,_____

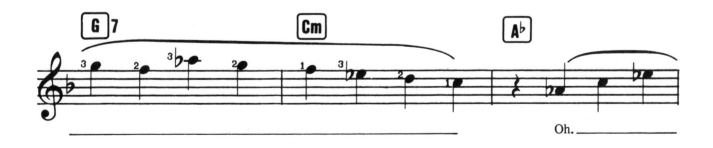

_____ Oh._____

So Nice

Music & original lyrics by
Marcos Valle & Paulo Sergio Valle
English Lyrics by Norman Gimbel

take my hand and sam - ba through life _____ with me.

Some - one to cling to me, Stay with me right _____ or wrong,

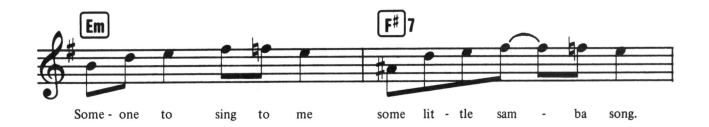

Some - one to sing to me some lit - tle sam - ba song.

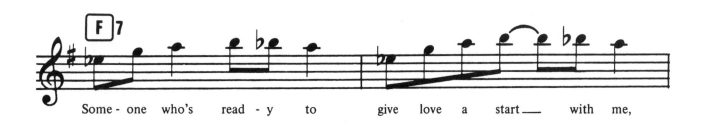

Some - one to take my heart, Then give his heart _____ to me,

Some - one who's read - y to give love a start _____ with me,

Oh yes, That would be So Nice, _____

Should it be you and me, I could see it would be nice. _____

It is often possible, and very effective, to play two or even three notes together in the right hand to enhance the melody of a song. Such supporting notes to the melody note must be carefully chosen, as they need to relate to the chord being played in your left hand.

What I Did For Love

Words by Edward Kleban
Music by Marvin Hamlisch

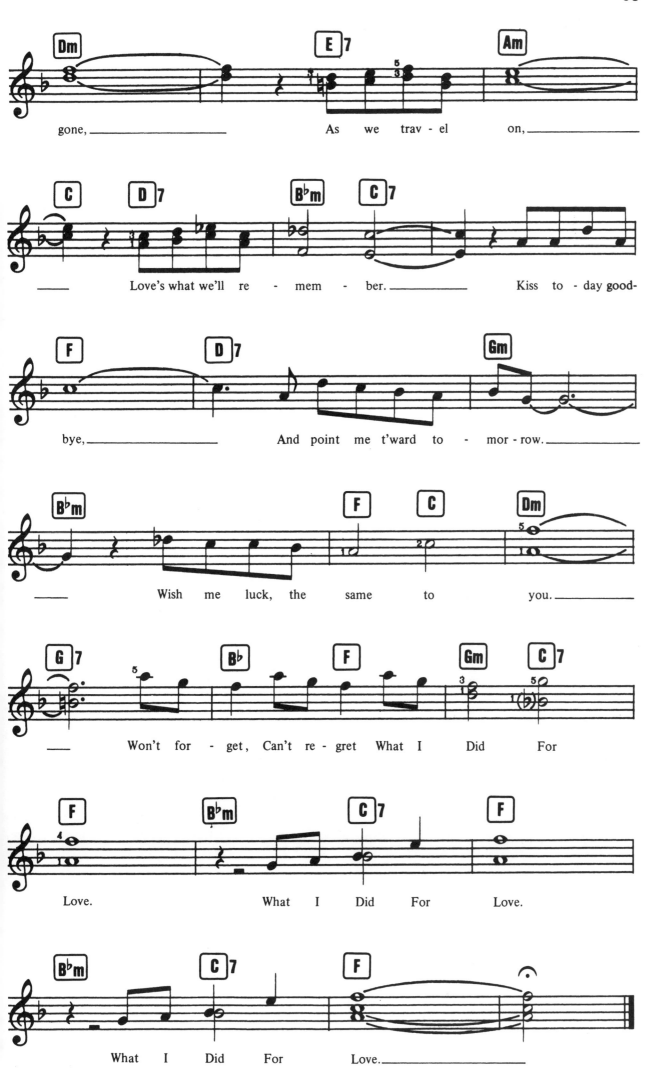

Augmented and Diminished Chords. Most keyboards are programmed for 'Fingered' chord accompaniment on the augmented and diminished chord forms.

These distinctive sounding chords are often used in popular music, and have their own symbols.

Example:

   C augmented: C aug, C+

   C diminished: C dim, C°

The chord shapes are easy to finger and learn on your keyboard.
Recurring patterns of equally spaced notes (intervals) in augmented and diminished chords result in groups of chord symbols having the same note structure:

Augmented Chords

C aug = E aug = G♯aug = A♭aug =

C♯aug = D♭aug = F aug = A aug =

D aug = F♯aug = G♭aug = A♯aug = B♭aug =

D♯aug = E♭aug = G aug = B aug =

Diminished Chords

C dim = D♯dim = E♭dim = F♯dim = G♭dim = A dim =

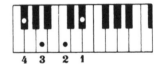

C♯dim = D♭dim = E dim = G dim = A♯dim = B♭dim =

D dim = F dim = G♯dim = A♭dim = B dim =

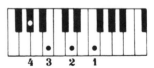

Augmented and diminished chords occasionally have numbers (5, 7,) included in the symbol. For left hand accompaniment purposes, these numbers may be disregarded; simply play the basic chord shape.